The Wright Guide to Mental Training

A Mental and Physical Fitness Log Book

ACKNOWLEDGMENTS

I wish to extend my appreciation to Jerry Braza, Jon Cary, Norm Eburne, and John Knight, faculty members of Western Oregon University. Thank you John MacDonald, and Portland State University writing laboratory, you inspired me. Special thanks to Geoffrey Kolstad, for all your hard work, efficiency, creativity, design ability and commitment to excellence. And to my lovely wife Lisa, thank you for encouraging me to go forward, your support, and love.

Available for purchase
by calling toll free 888-999-6168
or writing to: P.O. Box 19453, Portland, Oregon 97280

Table of Contents

INTRODUCTION

MENTAL TRAINING SKILLS PROGRAM

In recent years mental training has been identified as a breakthrough way of helping athletes achieve personal growth and peak performance through techniques of relaxation and mental imagery. Peak performance denotes a standard of accomplishment rather than a psychological state. Many elite athletes, coaches, and athletic program subscribe to mental training strategies.

RATIONALE

Traditionally it has been recognized that talent and physical attributes are the primary predictors of athletic potential. Most novice athletes are in this stage. However, athletes who tap into their mind, are best able to appreciate their own human potential. Physical ability alone will not produce peak performance, however, physical ability, physical preparedness, coupled with mental techniques can. Recently the coaching profession has become increasingly aware of the mind-body interdependence. Without a training approach that speaks to the athlete's mental attitude, as well as physical performance, less achievement is possible.

Mental training approaches include visualization, relaxation, goal setting, and positive thinking. If the athlete practices these techniques, he or she can improve concentration, increase calmness, confidence, and the ability to recognize and alleviate stress. Further, by consistently practicing these techniques, both in training, and in competition, the athlete is likely to achieve more consistent performance. The first and most important step in improving performance requires a consistent process of journaling training information. Therefore one should record all training information on a daily basis.

LITERATURE REVIEW

Sukey Waller (1995) defines peak performance as a "significant high point, a noticeable leap from a consistently high baseline level" (p.26). According to Waller, the two most important ingredients of peak performance are calmness and concentration. He asserts, that for maximum performance, the athlete must eliminate thoughts of fear, anger, failure and fatigue, during performance and the period prior to it. He points to the need to practice visualizing peak performance during and before competition. Visualization, argues Waller, should include minute details of form and strategy. As he puts it "pictures in the mind are very powerful" (p.26).

Orlick (1990) addresses the need to eliminate emotions of fear anger and failure which effect mood. He declares "its your mood, you can turn it around by thinking positive, happy, focused thoughts" (p.63). He asserts mood control is an element of mind control, and means "not upsetting yourself needlessly" (p.63).

Shane M. Murphy (1994) critically examined mental imagery research and intervention strategies as they relate to sports performance. Murphy concluded that these intervention strategies focus on four general categories: mental practice, precompetition, comparison of successful and unsuccessful competitors, and mediating variables. According to Murphy "mental imagery refers to all those sensory or perceptual experiences" (p. 491). He states that seeing an imagined performance routine, or feeling that " no grass or golf ball need to be present (p. 486)." These are examples of sensory and perceptual experience. He also notes that "99% of sample elite athletes use imagery techniques, of these elite athletes, 90% reported using mental imagery for training and competition (p. 486)." Many elite athletes believe a true state of relaxation is difficult to achieve without the use of mental strategy. Once the skill is acquired, elite athletes that were polled, said that "relaxation allows them to take giant steps toward optimal enjoyment and performance (486)."

Charles J. Hardy and Melissa A. Chase (1990) define relaxation as learning how to "let go and hang loose (p. 2)." They note that one needs to reach a certain degree of excitement in order to be fully invested in a given event, and thereby achieve optimal performance. However, too much excitement may interfere with an athlete's ability to focus on the task at hand, creating anxiety and inhibiting optimal performance. Hardy and Chase believe that the balance between excitement and relaxation focus is unique to each individual and each sport. Their research findings suggest that being calm helps the athlete develop heightened bodily sensitivity, and allows for the reduction of stress, which reduces muscular tension. Finally they believe that calmness and relaxation will help facilitate recovery from fatigue and promote restful sleep.

James P. Reardon (1995) believes that athletes often prepare adequately for competition, but ignore the attendant stress. He states that ignoring stress often results in a well trained, well prepared athlete who fails to perform to the level of his or her capability. Reardon, cited in Hans Selye, et al., acknowledges the ground breaking research on hormones and their relationship to stress. Selye was among the first to prove how stress effects human physiology. Selye concluded that "any problem or challenge, imagined or real, cause the cerebral cortex to send an alarm to the hypothalamus" (p 48). The hypothalamus then stimulates the sympathetic nervous system to make a series of changes in the body that affect heart rate, respiration, muscle tension, metabolism, blood pressure and blood distribution.

Herbert Benson (1975) found that by doing certain mental exercises, the brain can be quickly redirected to stop sending emergency signals to the brain stem, thereby stemming the panic messages that are sent to the nervous system. Benson defines this as the "fight-flight response" (p. 23). This response effects heart rate, breathing, muscle tension, and blood pressure. Breathing is also an important component in reducing muscle tension and relaxation. Williams (1992) states "breathing properly is not only relaxing, it facilitates performance by increasing the amount of oxygen in the blood. This carries more energy to the muscles and facilitates the removal of waste products" (p. 188). He adds "unfortunately, many individuals have never learned deep, diaphragmatic breathing, and those who have, often find their breathing patterns disrupted under stress" (p. 188).

In addition to Benson's claim, Reardon (1995) during an experiment, observed physical change during relaxation that shows a marked decrease in blood lactate. The reduction in blood lactate would seem to have a significant importance, it demonstrates a reduction of lactic acid in the muscle, a product associated with muscular tension, caused by anxiety or muscular work.

Reardon, explains that relaxation and imagery practice is most effective when it is interwoven into the physical training regime on a continual basis. He believes coaches should integrate concentration and calmness activities into the physical routine that include warm up, stretching and flexibility exercises at the beginning of practice. This will teach the athlete how to mentally transition from pre-practice activities, to narrowing their attention to the practice setting and focusing in on the training objective in a concentrated manner. Reardon recommends that athletes practice this until the process becomes effortless and automatic.

Csikszentmihalyi (1990) has studied components of peak performance or what he terms a "flow state (p. 54)." The results of Csikszentmihalyi study on flow state suggests that athletes need a challenging task requiring skill, the ability to concentrate on the process, rather than the outcome, clear goals, feedback, and a sense of control. These components, Csikszentmihlyi feels are the cornerstone of peak performance.

Jackson (1996) has studied components of "flow state" as well, defines flow as enjoyment (p.76). He alleges being able to attain flow during sport or exercise participation can elevate an experience to higher levels of "pleasure and achievement" (p.76-77).

Reardon (1992) talks about both the need for positive self-talk during imagery practice and rehearsal. Both help strengthen the neural pathways, which help form a mental blueprint, resulting in the mental mind set which readies the athlete for competition. One of the simplest of all the skills for improving concentration is positive self talk. When designing a mental imagery program Fred Surgent (1992) suggests including positive self-talk as part of the mental rehearsal practice, and when practicing mental rehearsal, be as detailed as possible.

Self-efficacy, defined by **Melissa Chase, Cathy D. Lirgg and Deborah L. Feltz (1997)** as a judgement about one's capability to successfully perform a task at a given level, is a reflection of the confidence level the athlete has in his or her self. And while an athlete's self efficacy impacts performance, coach's efficacy can impact performance as well. Chase, Lirgg, and Feltz, assert that it is generally understood that people will avoid situations they believe they are not capable of handling. Their level of efficacy will determine how much effort they put forth, and how long they persist in the face of failure. Chase, Lirgg and Feltz maintain that people with high self-efficacy can focus on the task at hand, people with low self-efficacy tend to divert from possible solution. They claim "individuals will tend to perform according to a superior's expectation, a phenomenon generally referred to as the" Pygmalion effect" (p. 9). They add "if a coach perceives the opponent to be of high ability, they would likely have lower team efficacy" (p. 10). Conversely, if past performances are successful efficacy expectation will increase.

Credit: Literature Review research by Alex Wright, MSED.

THE WRIGHT GUIDE FOR PEAK PERFORMANCE

Body Breathing Techniques
These techniques can be used to control pain, remove tension, and increase circulation to specific sites.

Long Breath Technique
While performing this technique, a person uses imagery to breath in and out of various parts of the body.

BODY BREATHING

STEP ONE: Which Type of Breather Are You?
- While lying on your back, place your hand high on your abdomen, just below the rib cage. Take a deep breath. As you do, notice the way your hand moves. Does it move up, down, not at all? If you

From, **Peak Performance,** Courtesy of Charles A. Garfield. © 1984 by Charles Garfield, by permission of Tarcher, Inc.; Los Angeles, California. Available in books.

are a diaphragmatic breather, your hand will move up, If you are a thoracic breather, your hand will move only slightly, if at all, or even down.

- Watch your hand as you breathe. Be aware of where most of the movement occurs, your chest, upper abdomen, lower abdomen, or all three.

STEP TWO: Focus On Your Abdomen
- Exhale, emptying your lungs completely.
- Take a deep breathe. As you inhale, place your hand on your abdomen and monitor the breathing patterns as follows:
- Lower abdomen expands, creating a vacuum in the chest cavity, causing air to be drawn into the lower lungs.
- As the middle section of the lungs fills, your upper abdomen expands.
- While you continue inhaling, your chest then expands, filling the upper regions of your lungs.

STEP THREE: Learn How You Breathe
- Exhale. Empty your lungs completely.
- Take a deep breath. Do you inhale through your nose or through your mouth?
- Exhale.
- Do you exhale through your nose or mouth?
- Mentally note your present breathing patterns before going on to the next step.

STEP FOUR: Correct Your Breathing
- Take a deep breath. This time, even if it is not your usual pattern, inhale through your nose, filling your lungs completely. Exhale through your mouth. Feel the warm air pass through your mouth and lips as you do.
- Follow this routine when ever you are breathing for relaxation.
- Inhale through your nose; exhale through your mouth.

Garfield, Charles A. (1984). Peak Performance.

STEP FIVE: Put it All Together
- Take a deep breath, inhaling through your nose.
- Watch your body as, first, your lower abdomen expands, then your upper abdomen, and finally your chest.
- Hold your breath for ten seconds.
- Feel the tension build in your throat and mouth as you hold your breath.
- Release your breath with a "sigh of relief," exhaling through your mouth.

MENTAL IMAGERY:

Imaging, the forming of mental pictures or images, is based on the principle that there is a deep tendency in human nature to become precisely like that which we imagine or image ourselves as being.

Imaging is positive thinking carried one step further. In imaging, one does not merely think about a hoped-for goal, one "sees" or visualizes it with tremendous intensity.

Imagery can be either internal or external. An internal perspective means that athletes see the image from behind their own eyes as if they were inside their bodies, as opposed to an external perspective in which they see the image from outside their bodies as a movie camera. Research has shown that elite athletes are more likely to practice imagery from an internal perspective as compared to non-elite athletes, who are more likely to practice imagery from an external perspective .

RELAXATION TECHNIQUE:

Garfield, Charles A. (1984). Peak Performance.

To achieve optimum performance on a regular basis, the ability to relax and control the tendency to become overaroused is necessary. But relaxation is more important to peak performance than just controlling this overaroused state. The benefits of relaxation for all athletes as well as for non-athletes are numerous. Listed below are some of the major benefits an athlete will derive from the ability to relax.

The major benefits of relaxation for athletes are:
Relaxation prepares one for mental imagery. Relaxation improves concentration ability. Relaxation helps control arousal level. Relaxation helps one sleep better. Relaxation helps improve body awareness.

In the following exercise, you will tense, and then relax certain muscle groups. Once you explore how you feel your muscles deliberately tensed and then relaxed, it is usually much easier to induce deep relaxation with the breathing and autogenic exercises that follow.

PREPARATION
Perform this exercise in a quiet place where you will not be disturbed for at least twenty minutes. With each step along way, pause for two or three seconds to be aware of your sensations and feelings. This exercise is to be done slowly and quietly. You will achieve optimal benefit if you sit in a straight, backed chair, since an alert, upright posture maintains a spinal alignment close to that used in classic, time-tested meditative postures.

INSTRUCTIONS
Step One
- Make a fist and squeeze firmly. Maintain the clenched position and trace your muscular involvement. Following only feelings, and without using words, note the sensations in your palm and fingers.

- Focus attention on the feelings in your wrist, the your hand, your forearm. Take your time. Be attentive to every sensation, no matter how subtle or insignificant it may seem.
- Again without using words, become aware of how your arm feels, your shoulder, your chest, your back.
- How does your clenched fist affect your breathing? Stomach muscles? Do you notice any tension, or any sensations, in your pelvis? Buttocks? Lower back?
- How do your legs feel? Do any sensations in you seem associated in any way with your fist?
- Release your clenched fist. Let your hand relax. Shake gently. Relax it. Shake it again. Relax it again.
- Now clench your fist once more.
- Make a mental note of any words that come to mind to describe the sensations you feel.
- Concentrate on your sensations as intensely as you can. To do this, use only single words to describe what you feel. Stop yourself if you have an impulse to find reasonable explanations for your feelings. Use single words only. Examples: *tight, contracted, prickly, hard, cold, strong, warm.* Responses are often highly individualized, and yours may or may not include any of the examples given.
- Make a mental note of simple words that come to mind to describe any emotions you are feeling, particularly those associated with your fist. Examples: *Resolute, fear, certainty, confusion.*
- Now completely relax your fist. Let your arm hang loosely at your side. Mentally note any physical sensations you are feeling while in this relaxed position, again using single words only. Examples: loose, light, tingling, warm. Pay close attention to subtle sensations. Follow these sensations over your musculature as you did when clenching your fist.

Garfield, Charles A. (1984). Peak Performance.

CONCENTRATION SKILLS:

Regardless of whether you are attempting to improve your ability to drop a putt on a quiet golf course, sink a free throw while hundreds of fans try to distract you, or hit a 90 m.p.h. fastball, the ability to concentrate, is a prerequisite to consistently high performance. However, as important as concentration is, very few athletes understand what it is. This creates a problem because if you don't understand what concentration is, how do you improve it?

First of all, concentration is a mental skill that like all other skills, can be perfected with practice. In sporting circles, concentration would best be defined as a narrowing or focusing of one's attention on a specific subject (task) to the exclusion of other subjects. Concentration can also be defined as a relaxed state of being mentally alert.

Many athletes have misconceptions that telling oneself to concentrate is the way to improve concentration. However, if you've got to remind yourself to concentrate during an athletic contest, you're not concentrating on the event, but you are concentrating on "trying to concentrate".

Another misconception about concentration is that the mind should never waver throughout the contest. This may be true in some, but not in all, sports. Concentration varies in both intensity and duration.

The key point to remember is that each person is different and you can develop your own successful style without emulating others.

Note:
In the past some Eastern European countries have used a concentration grid as a method for choosing their national teams.

GRID CONCENTRATION EXERCISE

Directions:
Beginning with 00, put a slash through each number in the proper sequence

84	27	51	78	59	52	13	85	61	55
28	60	92	04	97	90	31	57	29	33
32	96	65	39	80	77	49	86	18	70
76	87	71	95	98	81	01	46	88	00
48	82	89	47	35	17	10	42	62	34
44	67	93	11	07	43	72	94	69	56
53	79	05	22	54	74	58	14	91	02
06	68	99	75	26	15	41	66	20	40
50	09	64	08	38	30	36	45	83	24
03	73	21	23	16	37	25	19	12	63

Garfield, Charles A. (1984). Peak Performance.

AFFIRMATION FOR ATHLETIC PERFORMANCE

credit: Porter, Kay, Foster Jody (1986).
The Mental Athlete: Inner Training for Peak Performance. p. 149

I am a strong and fluid athlete.
I am as good as any other athlete at the competition today.
I am relaxed and ready to go.
My body is healthy and ready to go.
I am confident and ready.
I listen to my body and it serves me well.
I love my body.
I am powerful and balanced.
I am in control and focused.
I am the greatest.
I am a well trained and competent athlete.
I am performing pain free.
I am reaching my goal and realizing my peak.
I enjoy training and competing.
I enjoy being athletic and caring for my body.
I trust my body and its strength.
I am successful and winning.

Statements To Enhance Self-Image And Achieve A Positive Mental Attitude:

Every day in every way, I am better and better.
I am filled with love and kindness.
I am at peace with nature—and myself.
I am happy and content with my job.
I am a success.
Optimism makes me enthusiastic.

Statements To Alleviate Worry:

I live for the present.

This is a great day.
Problems are just opportunities in disguise.

STATEMENTS TO FOSTER RELAXATION, HEALTH, AND HEALING:

Affirmations For Fear and Self-doubt:
I am ready!
I am hot.
I hang in there.
I just do it.
I belong here.
It is easy for me to hear no.
I ask for what I want.
I am patient.
I handle rejection easily and turn it into something positive.
I learn from these experiences.
I am important.
What I say/need/want is important.
I am worthy of respect.
I trust and respect myself.
Affirmations For Feeling overwhelmed:
I am centered and relaxed.
I am strong, powerful, and centered.
I listen easy.
I am peaceful and harmonious in the midst of chaos.
I work on an even pace emotionally.

Porter, Kay, Foster Judy (1996). The Mental Athlete: Inner Training for Peak Performance. P.149

-WEEKLY PROGRESS CHART
-DAILY LOG
-DAILY MOOD CHART

WEEKLY PROGRESS MOOD CHART

Moods: ☺ ☺ 😐 🙁 ☹

WEEK:

	Beginning Mood	Ending Mood	Strategy Most Successful	Comments
Day				
1				
2				
3				
4				
5				
6				
7				

DAILY LOG

Monday
date
4 Jan

DAILY TOTAL 0

Tuesday
date
5 Jan

DAILY TOTAL 0

Wednesday
date
6 Jan

DAILY TOTAL 1

Thursday
date
7 Jan

DAILY TOTAL 3

Friday
date
8 Jan

DAILY TOTAL 3

Saturday
date
9 Jan

DAILY TOTAL 0

Sunday
date
10 Jan

gou trophy 1/2 marathon &
10'5 - 55:55 10'5
Straps slipped on foot plate

DAILY TOTAL 9

WEEKLY TOTAL MILES _____   TOTAL MINUTES _____
RESTING HR 80   EXERCISING HR _____   WEIGHT _____

WEEKLY PROGRESS MOOD CHART

Moods: ☺ ☺ ☺ ☹ ☹

WEEK:

Day	Beginning Mood	Ending Mood	Strategy Most Successful	Comments
1				
2				
3				
4				
5				
6				
7				

Weekly Mood Chart - From, **IN PURSUIT OF EXCELLENCE**, Courtesy of Tom Orlick. © 1990 by Tom Orlick. by permission of Human Kinetics; Champagne, Illinois. Available in books or call **(800) 747-4457**. $15.95 plus S&H

DAILY LOG

Monday
date
11 JAN 99

1½ mile regular chair

DAILY TOTAL

Tuesday
date

1½ mile reg chair

DAILY TOTAL

Wednesday
date

2 miles Reg Chair

DAILY TOTAL

Thursday
date

2 miles RC

DAILY TOTAL

Friday
date

2 miles RC

DAILY TOTAL

Saturday
date

DAILY TOTAL

Sunday
date

DAILY TOTAL

WEEKLY TOTAL MILES _____   TOTAL MINUTES _____
RESTING HR _____   EXERCISING HR _____   WEIGHT _____

WEEKLY PROGRESS MOOD CHART

Moods: 😊 😊 😐 🙁 ☹️

WEEK:

	Beginning Mood	Ending Mood	Strategy Most Successful	Comments
Day				
1				
2				
3				
4				
5				
6				
7				

DAILY LOG

Monday
date

DAILY TOTAL

Tuesday
date

DAILY TOTAL

Wednesday
date

DAILY TOTAL

Thursday
date

DAILY TOTAL

Friday
date

DAILY TOTAL

Saturday
date

DAILY TOTAL

Sunday
date

DAILY TOTAL

WEEKLY TOTAL MILES _____   TOTAL MINUTES _____

RESTING HR _____   EXERCISING HR _____   WEIGHT _____

WEEKLY PROGRESS MOOD CHART

Moods: ☺ ☺ ☺ ☹ ☹

WEEK:

Day	Beginning Mood	Ending Mood	Strategy Most Successful	Comments
1				
2				
3				
4				
5				
6				
7				

Weekly Mood Chart - From, **IN PURSUIT OF EXCELLENCE**, Courtesy of Tom Orlick. © 1990 by Tom Orlick. by permission of Human Kinetics; Champagne, Illinois. Available in books or call **(800) 747-4457**. $15.95 plus S&H

DAILY LOG

Monday
date

DAILY TOTAL

Tuesday
date

DAILY TOTAL

Wednesday
date

DAILY TOTAL

Thursday
date

DAILY TOTAL

Friday
date

DAILY TOTAL

Saturday
date

DAILY TOTAL

Sunday
date

DAILY TOTAL

WEEKLY TOTAL MILES _____   TOTAL MINUTES _____
RESTING HR _____   EXERCISING HR _____   WEIGHT _____

WEEKLY PROGRESS MOOD CHART

Moods: ☺ ☺ ☺ ☹ ☹

WEEK:

	Beginning Mood	Ending Mood	Strategy Most Successful	Comments
Day				
1				
2				
3				
4				
5				
6				
7				

Weekly Mood Chart - From, **IN PURSUIT OF EXCELLENCE**, Courtesy of Tom Orlick. © 1990 by Tom Orlick. by permission of Human Kinetics; Champagne, Illinois. Available in books or call **(800) 747-4457**. $15.95 plus S&H

DAILY LOG

Monday
date

DAILY TOTAL

Tuesday
date

DAILY TOTAL

Wednesday
date

DAILY TOTAL

Thursday
date

DAILY TOTAL

Friday
date

DAILY TOTAL

Saturday
date

DAILY TOTAL

Sunday
date

DAILY TOTAL

WEEKLY TOTAL MILES _____ **TOTAL MINUTES** _____

RESTING HR _____ **EXERCISING HR** _____ **WEIGHT** _____

WEEKLY PROGRESS MOOD CHART

Moods: ☺ ☺ ☺ ☹ ☹

WEEK:

	Beginning Mood	Ending Mood	Strategy Most Successful	Comments
Day				
1				
2				
3				
4				
5				
6				
7				

Weekly Mood Chart - From, **IN PURSUIT OF EXCELLENCE**, Courtesy of Tom Orlick. © 1990 by Tom Orlick. by permission of Human Kinetics; Champagne, Illinois. Available in books or call **(800) 747-4457**. $15.95 plus S&H

DAILY LOG

Monday
date

DAILY TOTAL

Tuesday
date

DAILY TOTAL

Wednesday
date

DAILY TOTAL

Thursday
date

DAILY TOTAL

Friday
date

DAILY TOTAL

Saturday
date

DAILY TOTAL

Sunday
date

DAILY TOTAL

WEEKLY TOTAL MILES _____   TOTAL MINUTES _____

RESTING HR _____   EXERCISING HR _____   WEIGHT _____

WEEKLY PROGRESS MOOD CHART

Moods: ☺ 🙂 😐 🙁 ☹

WEEK:

	Beginning Mood	Ending Mood	Strategy Most Successful	Comments
Day				
1				
2				
3				
4				
5				
6				
7				

DAILY LOG

Monday
date

DAILY TOTAL

Tuesday
date

DAILY TOTAL

Wednesday
date

DAILY TOTAL

Thursday
date

DAILY TOTAL

Friday
date

DAILY TOTAL

Saturday
date

DAILY TOTAL

Sunday
date

DAILY TOTAL

WEEKLY TOTAL MILES _____   TOTAL MINUTES _____
RESTING HR _____   EXERCISING HR _____   WEIGHT _____

WEEKLY PROGRESS MOOD CHART

Moods: ☺ ☺ ☺ ☹ ☹

WEEK:

Day	Beginning Mood	Ending Mood	Strategy Most Successful	Comments
1				
2				
3				
4				
5				
6				
7				

Weekly Mood Chart - From, **IN PURSUIT OF EXCELLENCE,** Courtesy of Tom Orlick. © 1990 by Tom Orlick. by permission of Human Kinetics; Champagne, Illinois. Available in books or call **(800) 747-4457.** $15.95 plus S&H

DAILY LOG

Monday
date

DAILY TOTAL

Tuesday
date

DAILY TOTAL

Wednesday
date

DAILY TOTAL

Thursday
date

DAILY TOTAL

Friday
date

DAILY TOTAL

Saturday
date

DAILY TOTAL

Sunday
date

DAILY TOTAL

WEEKLY TOTAL MILES _____   TOTAL MINUTES _____
        RESTING HR _____   EXERCISING HR _____   WEIGHT _____

WEEKLY PROGRESS MOOD CHART

Moods: ☺ ☺ ☺ ☹ ☹

WEEK:

	Beginning Mood	Ending Mood	Strategy Most Successful	Comments
Day				
1				
2				
3				
4				
5				
6				
7				

Weekly Mood Chart - From, __IN PURSUIT OF EXCELLENCE__, Courtesy of Tom Orlick. © 1990 by Tom Orlick. by permission of Human Kinetics; Champagne, Illinois. Available in books or call **(800) 747-4457**. $15.95 plus S&H

DAILY LOG

Monday
date

DAILY TOTAL

Tuesday
date

DAILY TOTAL

Wednesday
date

DAILY TOTAL

Thursday
date

DAILY TOTAL

Friday
date

DAILY TOTAL

Saturday
date

DAILY TOTAL

Sunday
date

DAILY TOTAL

WEEKLY TOTAL MILES _____   TOTAL MINUTES _____

RESTING HR _____   EXERCISING HR _____   WEIGHT _____

WEEKLY PROGRESS MOOD CHART

Moods: ☺ ☺ ☺ ☹ ☹

WEEK:

	Beginning Mood	Ending Mood	Strategy Most Successful	Comments
Day				
1				
2				
3				
4				
5				
6				
7				

DAILY LOG

Monday
date

DAILY TOTAL

Tuesday
date

DAILY TOTAL

Wednesday
date

DAILY TOTAL

Thursday
date

DAILY TOTAL

Friday
date

DAILY TOTAL

Saturday
date

DAILY TOTAL

Sunday
date

DAILY TOTAL

WEEKLY TOTAL MILES _____   TOTAL MINUTES _____

RESTING HR _____   EXERCISING HR _____   WEIGHT _____

WEEKLY PROGRESS MOOD CHART

Moods: 😊 😊 😐 ☹️ ☹️

WEEK:

	Beginning Mood	Ending Mood	Strategy Most Successful	Comments
Day				
1				
2				
3				
4				
5				
6				
7				

Weekly Mood Chart - From, **IN PURSUIT OF EXCELLENCE**, Courtesy of Tom Orlick. © 1990 by Tom Orlick. by permission of Human Kinetics; Champagne, Illinois. Available in books or call **(800) 747-4457**. $15.95 plus S&H

DAILY LOG

Monday
date

DAILY TOTAL

Tuesday
date

DAILY TOTAL

Wednesday
date

DAILY TOTAL

Thursday
date

DAILY TOTAL

Friday
date

DAILY TOTAL

Saturday
date

DAILY TOTAL

Sunday
date

DAILY TOTAL

WEEKLY TOTAL MILES _____   TOTAL MINUTES _____
          RESTING HR _____   EXERCISING HR _____   WEIGHT _____

WEEKLY PROGRESS MOOD CHART

Moods: ☺ ☺ 😐 🙁 🙁

WEEK:

	Beginning Mood	Ending Mood	Strategy Most Successful	Comments
Day				
1				
2				
3				
4				
5				
6				
7				

Weekly Mood Chart - From, **IN PURSUIT OF EXCELLENCE,** Courtesy of Tom Orlick. © 1990 by Tom Orlick. by permission of Human Kinetics; Champagne, Illinois. Available in books or call **(800) 747-4457.** $15.95 plus S&H

DAILY LOG

Monday
date

DAILY TOTAL

Tuesday
date

DAILY TOTAL

Wednesday
date

DAILY TOTAL

Thursday
date

DAILY TOTAL

Friday
date

DAILY TOTAL

Saturday
date

DAILY TOTAL

Sunday
date

DAILY TOTAL

WEEKLY TOTAL MILES _____   TOTAL MINUTES _____
RESTING HR _____   EXERCISING HR _____   WEIGHT _____

WEEKLY PROGRESS MOOD CHART

Moods:	☺ ☺ ☺ ☹ ☹

WEEK:

Day	Beginning Mood	Ending Mood	Strategy Most Successful	Comments
1				
2				
3				
4				
5				
6				
7				

Weekly Mood Chart - From, **IN PURSUIT OF EXCELLENCE,** Courtesy of Tom Orlick. © 1990 by Tom Orlick. by permission of Human Kinetics; Champagne, Illinois. Available in books or call **(800) 747-4457.** $15.95 plus S&H

DAILY LOG

Monday
date

DAILY TOTAL

Tuesday
date

DAILY TOTAL

Wednesday
date

DAILY TOTAL

Thursday
date

DAILY TOTAL

Friday
date

DAILY TOTAL

Saturday
date

DAILY TOTAL

Sunday
date

DAILY TOTAL

WEEKLY TOTAL MILES _____   TOTAL MINUTES _____
        RESTING HR _____   EXERCISING HR _____   WEIGHT _____

WEEKLY PROGRESS MOOD CHART

| Moods: | ☺ | ☺ | 😐 | ☹ | ☹ |

WEEK:

	Beginning Mood	Ending Mood	Strategy Most Successful	Comments
Day				
1				
2				
3				
4				
5				
6				
7				

DAILY LOG

Monday
date

DAILY TOTAL

Tuesday
date

DAILY TOTAL

Wednesday
date

DAILY TOTAL

Thursday
date

DAILY TOTAL

Friday
date

DAILY TOTAL

Saturday
date

DAILY TOTAL

Sunday
date

DAILY TOTAL

WEEKLY TOTAL MILES _____   TOTAL MINUTES _____

RESTING HR _____   EXERCISING HR _____   WEIGHT _____

WEEKLY PROGRESS MOOD CHART

Moods:	😊 😊 😐 🙁 🙁

WEEK:

Day	Beginning Mood	Ending Mood	Strategy Most Successful	Comments
1				
2				
3				
4				
5				
6				
7				

DAILY LOG

Monday
date

DAILY TOTAL

Tuesday
date

DAILY TOTAL

Wednesday
date

DAILY TOTAL

Thursday
date

DAILY TOTAL

Friday
date

DAILY TOTAL

Saturday
date

DAILY TOTAL

Sunday
date

DAILY TOTAL

WEEKLY TOTAL MILES _____   TOTAL MINUTES _____
RESTING HR _____   EXERCISING HR _____   WEIGHT _____

WEEKLY PROGRESS MOOD CHART

Moods:	☺ ☺ 😐 🙁 ☹

WEEK:

	Beginning Mood	Ending Mood	Strategy Most Successful	Comments
Day				
1				
2				
3				
4				
5				
6				
7				

DAILY LOG

Monday
date

DAILY TOTAL

Tuesday
date

DAILY TOTAL

Wednesday
date

DAILY TOTAL

Thursday
date

DAILY TOTAL

Friday
date

DAILY TOTAL

Saturday
date

DAILY TOTAL

Sunday
date

DAILY TOTAL

WEEKLY TOTAL MILES _____   TOTAL MINUTES _____

RESTING HR _____   EXERCISING HR _____   WEIGHT _____

WEEKLY PROGRESS MOOD CHART

Moods: ☺ ☺ ☺ ☹ ☹

WEEK:

	Beginning Mood	Ending Mood	Strategy Most Successful	Comments
Day				
1				
2				
3				
4				
5				
6				
7				

DAILY LOG

Monday
date

DAILY TOTAL

Tuesday
date

DAILY TOTAL

Wednesday
date

DAILY TOTAL

Thursday
date

DAILY TOTAL

Friday
date

DAILY TOTAL

Saturday
date

DAILY TOTAL

Sunday
date

DAILY TOTAL

WEEKLY TOTAL MILES _____   TOTAL MINUTES _____

RESTING HR _____   EXERCISING HR _____   WEIGHT _____

WEEKLY PROGRESS MOOD CHART

Moods: ☺ ☺ ☺ ☹ ☹

WEEK:

	Beginning Mood	Ending Mood	Strategy Most Successful	Comments
Day				
1				
2				
3				
4				
5				
6				
7				

Weekly Mood Chart - From, **IN PURSUIT OF EXCELLENCE**, Courtesy of Tom Orlick. © 1990 by Tom Orlick. by permission of Human Kinetics; Champagne, Illinois. Available in books or call **(800) 747-4457**. $15.95 plus S&H

DAILY LOG

Monday
date

DAILY TOTAL

Tuesday
date

DAILY TOTAL

Wednesday
date

DAILY TOTAL

Thursday
date

DAILY TOTAL

Friday
date

DAILY TOTAL

Saturday
date

DAILY TOTAL

Sunday
date

DAILY TOTAL

WEEKLY TOTAL MILES _____   TOTAL MINUTES _____

RESTING HR _____   EXERCISING HR _____   WEIGHT _____

WEEKLY PROGRESS MOOD CHART

Moods: ☺ ☺ ☺ ☹ ☹

WEEK:

Day	Beginning Mood	Ending Mood	Strategy Most Successful	Comments
1				
2				
3				
4				
5				
6				
7				

Weekly Mood Chart - From, **IN PURSUIT OF EXCELLENCE**, Courtesy of Tom Orlick. © 1990 by Tom Orlick. by permission of Human Kinetics; Champagne, Illinois. Available in books or call **(800) 747-4457**. $15.95 plus S&H

DAILY LOG

Monday
date

DAILY TOTAL

Tuesday
date

DAILY TOTAL

Wednesday
date

DAILY TOTAL

Thursday
date

DAILY TOTAL

Friday
date

DAILY TOTAL

Saturday
date

DAILY TOTAL

Sunday
date

DAILY TOTAL

WEEKLY TOTAL MILES _____   TOTAL MINUTES _____

RESTING HR _____   EXERCISING HR _____   WEIGHT _____

WEEKLY PROGRESS MOOD CHART

Moods: 😊 🙂 😐 🙁 ☹️

WEEK:

Day	Beginning Mood	Ending Mood	Strategy Most Successful	Comments
1				
2				
3				
4				
5				
6				
7				

Weekly Mood Chart - From, **IN PURSUIT OF EXCELLENCE,** Courtesy of Tom Orlick. © 1990 by Tom Orlick. by permission of Human Kinetics; Champagne, Illinois. Available in books or call **(800) 747-4457.** $15.95 plus S&H

DAILY LOG

Monday
date

DAILY TOTAL

Tuesday
date

DAILY TOTAL

Wednesday
date

DAILY TOTAL

Thursday
date

DAILY TOTAL

Friday
date

DAILY TOTAL

Saturday
date

DAILY TOTAL

Sunday
date

DAILY TOTAL

WEEKLY TOTAL MILES _____   TOTAL MINUTES _____

RESTING HR _____   EXERCISING HR _____   WEIGHT _____

WEEKLY PROGRESS MOOD CHART

Moods:	☺	☺	☺	☹	☹

WEEK:

	Beginning Mood	Ending Mood	Strategy Most Successful	Comments
Day				
1				
2				
3				
4				
5				
6				
7				

DAILY LOG

Monday
date

DAILY TOTAL

Tuesday
date

DAILY TOTAL

Wednesday
date

DAILY TOTAL

Thursday
date

DAILY TOTAL

Friday
date

DAILY TOTAL

Saturday
date

DAILY TOTAL

Sunday
date

DAILY TOTAL

WEEKLY TOTAL MILES _____   TOTAL MINUTES _____
            RESTING HR _____   EXERCISING HR _____   WEIGHT _____

WEEKLY PROGRESS MOOD CHART

| Moods: | ☺ | ☺ | ☺ | ☹ | ☹ |

WEEK:

	Beginning Mood	Ending Mood	Strategy Most Successful	Comments
Day				
1				
2				
3				
4				
5				
6				
7				

DAILY LOG

Monday
date

DAILY TOTAL

Tuesday
date

DAILY TOTAL

Wednesday
date

DAILY TOTAL

Thursday
date

DAILY TOTAL

Friday
date

DAILY TOTAL

Saturday
date

DAILY TOTAL

Sunday
date

DAILY TOTAL

WEEKLY TOTAL MILES _____   TOTAL MINUTES _____

RESTING HR _____   EXERCISING HR _____   WEIGHT _____

WEEKLY PROGRESS MOOD CHART

Moods:

	Beginning Mood	Ending Mood	Strategy Most Successful	Comments
WEEK:				
Day				
1				
2				
3				
4				
5				
6				
7				

Weekly Mood Chart - From, **IN PURSUIT OF EXCELLENCE**, Courtesy of Tom Orlick. © 1990 by Tom Orlick. by permission of Human Kinetics; Champagne, Illinois. Available in books or call **(800) 747-4457**. $15.95 plus S&H

DAILY LOG

Monday
date

DAILY TOTAL

Tuesday
date

DAILY TOTAL

Wednesday
date

DAILY TOTAL

Thursday
date

DAILY TOTAL

Friday
date

DAILY TOTAL

Saturday
date

DAILY TOTAL

Sunday
date

DAILY TOTAL

WEEKLY TOTAL MILES _____   **TOTAL MINUTES** _____

RESTING HR _____   **EXERCISING HR** _____   **WEIGHT** _____

WEEKLY PROGRESS MOOD CHART

Moods: ☺ ☺ ☺ ☹ ☹

WEEK:

	Beginning Mood	Ending Mood	Strategy Most Successful	Comments
Day				
1				
2				
3				
4				
5				
6				
7				

Weekly Mood Chart - From, **IN PURSUIT OF EXCELLENCE**, Courtesy of Tom Orlick. © 1990 by Tom Orlick. by permission of Human Kinetics; Champagne, Illinois. Available in books or call **(800) 747-4457**. $15.95 plus S&H

DAILY LOG

Monday
date

DAILY TOTAL

Tuesday
date

DAILY TOTAL

Wednesday
date

DAILY TOTAL

Thursday
date

DAILY TOTAL

Friday
date

DAILY TOTAL

Saturday
date

DAILY TOTAL

Sunday
date

DAILY TOTAL

WEEKLY TOTAL MILES _____   TOTAL MINUTES _____

RESTING HR _____   EXERCISING HR _____   WEIGHT _____

WEEKLY PROGRESS MOOD CHART

Moods: ☺ ☺ ☺ ☹ ☹

WEEK:

	Beginning Mood	Ending Mood	Strategy Most Successful	Comments
Day				
1				
2				
3				
4				
5				
6				
7				

Weekly Mood Chart - From, **IN PURSUIT OF EXCELLENCE,** Courtesy of Tom Orlick. © 1990 by Tom Orlick. by permission of Human Kinetics; Champagne, Illinois. Available in books or call **(800) 747-4457.** $15.95 plus S&H

DAILY LOG

Monday
date

DAILY TOTAL

Tuesday
date

DAILY TOTAL

Wednesday
date

DAILY TOTAL

Thursday
date

DAILY TOTAL

Friday
date

DAILY TOTAL

Saturday
date

DAILY TOTAL

Sunday
date

DAILY TOTAL

WEEKLY TOTAL MILES _____   TOTAL MINUTES _____
RESTING HR _____   EXERCISING HR _____   WEIGHT _____

WEEKLY PROGRESS MOOD CHART

Moods: ☺ ☺ ☺ ☹ ☹

WEEK:

	Beginning Mood	Ending Mood	Strategy Most Successful	Comments
Day				
1				
2				
3				
4				
5				
6				
7				

DAILY LOG

Monday
date

DAILY TOTAL

Tuesday
date

DAILY TOTAL

Wednesday
date

DAILY TOTAL

Thursday
date

DAILY TOTAL

Friday
date

DAILY TOTAL

Saturday
date

DAILY TOTAL

Sunday
date

DAILY TOTAL

WEEKLY TOTAL MILES _____   TOTAL MINUTES _____
RESTING HR _____   EXERCISING HR _____   WEIGHT _____

WEEKLY PROGRESS MOOD CHART

Moods:	☺ ☺ ☺ ☹ ☹

WEEK:

	Beginning Mood	Ending Mood	Strategy Most Successful	Comments
Day				
1				
2				
3				
4				
5				
6				
7				

Weekly Mood Chart - From, __IN PURSUIT OF EXCELLENCE__, Courtesy of Tom Orlick. © 1990 by Tom Orlick. by permission of Human Kinetics; Champagne, Illinois. Available in books or call **(800) 747-4457**. $15.95 plus S&H

DAILY LOG

Monday
date

DAILY TOTAL

Tuesday
date

DAILY TOTAL

Wednesday
date

DAILY TOTAL

Thursday
date

DAILY TOTAL

Friday
date

DAILY TOTAL

Saturday
date

DAILY TOTAL

Sunday
date

DAILY TOTAL

WEEKLY TOTAL MILES _____   TOTAL MINUTES _____

RESTING HR _____   EXERCISING HR _____   WEIGHT _____

WEEKLY PROGRESS MOOD CHART

Moods: ☺ ☺ ☺ ☹ ☹

WEEK:

Day	Beginning Mood	Ending Mood	Strategy Most Successful	Comments
1				
2				
3				
4				
5				
6				
7				

DAILY LOG

Monday
date

DAILY TOTAL

Tuesday
date

DAILY TOTAL

Wednesday
date

DAILY TOTAL

Thursday
date

DAILY TOTAL

Friday
date

DAILY TOTAL

Saturday
date

DAILY TOTAL

Sunday
date

DAILY TOTAL

WEEKLY TOTAL MILES _____   TOTAL MINUTES _____

RESTING HR _____   EXERCISING HR _____   WEIGHT _____

WEEKLY PROGRESS MOOD CHART

Moods: 🙂 😊 😐 🙁 😦

WEEK:

Day	Beginning Mood	Ending Mood	Strategy Most Successful	Comments
1				
2				
3				
4				
5				
6				
7				

Weekly Mood Chart - From, **IN PURSUIT OF EXCELLENCE,** Courtesy of Tom Orlick. © 1990 by Tom Orlick. by permission of Human Kinetics; Champagne, Illinois. Available in books or call **(800) 747-4457.** $15.95 plus S&H

DAILY LOG

Monday
date

DAILY TOTAL

Tuesday
date

DAILY TOTAL

Wednesday
date

DAILY TOTAL

Thursday
date

DAILY TOTAL

Friday
date

DAILY TOTAL

Saturday
date

DAILY TOTAL

Sunday
date

DAILY TOTAL

WEEKLY TOTAL MILES _____   TOTAL MINUTES _____
        RESTING HR _____   EXERCISING HR _____   WEIGHT _____

WEEKLY PROGRESS MOOD CHART

| Moods: | ☺ | ☺ | 😐 | ☹ | ☹ |

WEEK:

	Beginning Mood	Ending Mood	Strategy Most Successful	Comments
Day				
1				
2				
3				
4				
5				
6				
7				

DAILY LOG

Monday
date

DAILY TOTAL

Tuesday
date

DAILY TOTAL

Wednesday
date

DAILY TOTAL

Thursday
date

DAILY TOTAL

Friday
date

DAILY TOTAL

Saturday
date

DAILY TOTAL

Sunday
date

DAILY TOTAL

WEEKLY TOTAL MILES _____   TOTAL MINUTES _____

RESTING HR _____   EXERCISING HR _____   WEIGHT _____

WEEKLY PROGRESS MOOD CHART

Moods:	☺ ☺ 😐 🙁 ☹

WEEK:

	Beginning Mood	Ending Mood	Strategy Most Successful	Comments
Day				
1				
2				
3				
4				
5				
6				
7				

Weekly Mood Chart - From, **IN PURSUIT OF EXCELLENCE,** Courtesy of Tom Orlick. © 1990 by Tom Orlick. by permission of Human Kinetics; Champagne, Illinois. Available in books or call **(800) 747-4457.** $15.95 plus S&H

DAILY LOG

Monday
date

DAILY TOTAL

Tuesday
date

DAILY TOTAL

Wednesday
date

DAILY TOTAL

Thursday
date

DAILY TOTAL

Friday
date

DAILY TOTAL

Saturday
date

DAILY TOTAL

Sunday
date

DAILY TOTAL

WEEKLY TOTAL MILES _____   TOTAL MINUTES_____
RESTING HR _____   EXERCISING HR_____   WEIGHT _____

WEEKLY PROGRESS MOOD CHART

Moods: ☺ 😐 😐 🙁 ☹

WEEK:

	Beginning Mood	Ending Mood	Strategy Most Successful	Comments
Day				
1				
2				
3				
4				
5				
6				
7				

Weekly Mood Chart - From, **IN PURSUIT OF EXCELLENCE**, Courtesy of Tom Orlick. © 1990 by Tom Orlick. by permission of Human Kinetics; Champagne, Illinois. Available in books or call **(800) 747-4457.** $15.95 plus S&H

DAILY LOG

Monday
date

DAILY TOTAL

Tuesday
date

DAILY TOTAL

Wednesday
date

DAILY TOTAL

Thursday
date

DAILY TOTAL

Friday
date

DAILY TOTAL

Saturday
date

DAILY TOTAL

Sunday
date

DAILY TOTAL

WEEKLY TOTAL MILES _____   TOTAL MINUTES _____
RESTING HR _____   EXERCISING HR _____   WEIGHT _____

WEEKLY PROGRESS MOOD CHART

Moods: ☺ ☺ ☺ ☹ ☹

WEEK:

	Beginning Mood	Ending Mood	Strategy Most Successful	Comments
Day				
1				
2				
3				
4				
5				
6				
7				

Weekly Mood Chart - From, **IN PURSUIT OF EXCELLENCE**, Courtesy of Tom Orlick. © 1990 by Tom Orlick. by permission of Human Kinetics; Champagne, Illinois. Available in books or call **(800) 747-4457**. $15.95 plus S&H

DAILY LOG

Monday
date

DAILY TOTAL

Tuesday
date

DAILY TOTAL

Wednesday
date

DAILY TOTAL

Thursday
date

DAILY TOTAL

Friday
date

DAILY TOTAL

Saturday
date

DAILY TOTAL

Sunday
date

DAILY TOTAL

WEEKLY TOTAL MILES _____   TOTAL MINUTES _____

RESTING HR _____   EXERCISING HR _____   WEIGHT _____

WEEKLY PROGRESS MOOD CHART

Moods: ☺ ☺ 😐 ☹ ☹

WEEK:

	Beginning Mood	Ending Mood	Strategy Most Successful	Comments
Day				
1				
2				
3				
4				
5				
6				
7				

DAILY LOG

Monday
date

DAILY TOTAL

Tuesday
date

DAILY TOTAL

Wednesday
date

DAILY TOTAL

Thursday
date

DAILY TOTAL

Friday
date

DAILY TOTAL

Saturday
date

DAILY TOTAL

Sunday
date

DAILY TOTAL

WEEKLY TOTAL MILES _____   TOTAL MINUTES _____
RESTING HR _____   EXERCISING HR _____   WEIGHT _____

WEEKLY PROGRESS MOOD CHART

Moods: ☺ ☺ ☺ ☹ ☹

WEEK:

	Beginning Mood	Ending Mood	Strategy Most Successful	Comments
Day				
1				
2				
3				
4				
5				
6				
7				

DAILY LOG

Monday
date

DAILY TOTAL

Tuesday
date

DAILY TOTAL

Wednesday
date

DAILY TOTAL

Thursday
date

DAILY TOTAL

Friday
date

DAILY TOTAL

Saturday
date

DAILY TOTAL

Sunday
date

DAILY TOTAL

WEEKLY TOTAL MILES _____   TOTAL MINUTES _____

RESTING HR _____   EXERCISING HR _____   WEIGHT _____

WEEKLY PROGRESS MOOD CHART

Moods: 😊 😊 😐 🙁 😦

WEEK:

Day	Beginning Mood	Ending Mood	Strategy Most Successful	Comments
1				
2				
3				
4				
5				
6				
7				

DAILY LOG

Monday
date

DAILY TOTAL

Tuesday
date

DAILY TOTAL

Wednesday
date

DAILY TOTAL

Thursday
date

DAILY TOTAL

Friday
date

DAILY TOTAL

Saturday
date

DAILY TOTAL

Sunday
date

DAILY TOTAL

WEEKLY TOTAL MILES _____   TOTAL MINUTES _____

RESTING HR _____   EXERCISING HR _____   WEIGHT _____

WEEKLY PROGRESS MOOD CHART

Moods: ☺ 😐 😐 ☹ ☹

WEEK:

	Beginning Mood	Ending Mood	Strategy Most Successful	Comments
Day				
1				
2				
3				
4				
5				
6				
7				

Weekly Mood Chart - From, **IN PURSUIT OF EXCELLENCE**, Courtesy of Tom Orlick. © 1990 by Tom Orlick. by permission of Human Kinetics; Champagne, Illinois. Available in books or call **(800) 747-4457**. $15.95 plus S&H

DAILY LOG

Monday
date

DAILY TOTAL

Tuesday
date

DAILY TOTAL

Wednesday
date

DAILY TOTAL

Thursday
date

DAILY TOTAL

Friday
date

DAILY TOTAL

Saturday
date

DAILY TOTAL

Sunday
date

DAILY TOTAL

WEEKLY TOTAL MILES _____   TOTAL MINUTES _____

RESTING HR _____   EXERCISING HR _____   WEIGHT _____

WEEKLY PROGRESS MOOD CHART

Moods: / ☺ ☺ ☺ ☺ ☺

WEEK:

	Beginning Mood	Ending Mood	Strategy Most Successful	Comments
Day				
1				
2				
3				
4				
5				
6				
7				

DAILY LOG

Monday
date

DAILY TOTAL

Tuesday
date

DAILY TOTAL

Wednesday
date

DAILY TOTAL

Thursday
date

DAILY TOTAL

Friday
date

DAILY TOTAL

Saturday
date

DAILY TOTAL

Sunday
date

DAILY TOTAL

WEEKLY TOTAL MILES _____ TOTAL MINUTES _____

RESTING HR _____ EXERCISING HR _____ WEIGHT _____

WEEKLY PROGRESS MOOD CHART

Moods: ☺ ☺ ☺ ☹ ☹

WEEK:

	Beginning Mood	Ending Mood	Strategy Most Successful	Comments
Day				
1				
2				
3				
4				
5				
6				
7				

DAILY LOG

Monday
date

DAILY TOTAL

Tuesday
date

DAILY TOTAL

Wednesday
date

DAILY TOTAL

Thursday
date

DAILY TOTAL

Friday
date

DAILY TOTAL

Saturday
date

DAILY TOTAL

Sunday
date

DAILY TOTAL

WEEKLY TOTAL MILES _____   TOTAL MINUTES _____

RESTING HR _____   EXERCISING HR _____   WEIGHT _____

WEEKLY PROGRESS MOOD CHART

Moods: ☺ ☺ 😐 🙁 ☹

WEEK:

Day	Beginning Mood	Ending Mood	Strategy Most Successful	Comments
1				
2				
3				
4				
5				
6				
7				

DAILY LOG

Monday
date

DAILY TOTAL

Tuesday
date

DAILY TOTAL

Wednesday
date

DAILY TOTAL

Thursday
date

DAILY TOTAL

Friday
date

DAILY TOTAL

Saturday
date

DAILY TOTAL

Sunday
date

DAILY TOTAL

WEEKLY TOTAL MILES _____   TOTAL MINUTES _____
RESTING HR _____   EXERCISING HR _____   WEIGHT _____

WEEKLY PROGRESS MOOD CHART

Moods: ☺ ☺ ☺ ☹ ☹

WEEK:

	Beginning Mood	Ending Mood	Strategy Most Successful	Comments
Day				
1				
2				
3				
4				
5				
6				
7				

Weekly Mood Chart - From, __IN PURSUIT OF EXCELLENCE__, Courtesy of Tom Orlick. © 1990 by Tom Orlick. by permission of Human Kinetics; Champagne, Illinois. Available in books or call **(800) 747-4457**. $15.95 plus S&H

DAILY LOG

Monday
date

DAILY TOTAL

Tuesday
date

DAILY TOTAL

Wednesday
date

DAILY TOTAL

Thursday
date

DAILY TOTAL

Friday
date

DAILY TOTAL

Saturday
date

DAILY TOTAL

Sunday
date

DAILY TOTAL

WEEKLY TOTAL MILES _____   TOTAL MINUTES _____

RESTING HR _____   EXERCISING HR _____   WEIGHT _____

WEEKLY PROGRESS MOOD CHART

Moods: ☺ ☻ 😐 🙁 ☹

WEEK:

Day	Beginning Mood	Ending Mood	Strategy Most Successful	Comments
1				
2				
3				
4				
5				
6				
7				

Weekly Mood Chart - From, **IN PURSUIT OF EXCELLENCE**, Courtesy of Tom Orlick. © 1990 by Tom Orlick. by permission of Human Kinetics; Champagne, Illinois. Available in books or call **(800) 747-4457**. $15.95 plus S&H

DAILY LOG

Monday
date

DAILY TOTAL

Tuesday
date

DAILY TOTAL

Wednesday
date

DAILY TOTAL

Thursday
date

DAILY TOTAL

Friday
date

DAILY TOTAL

Saturday
date

DAILY TOTAL

Sunday
date

DAILY TOTAL

WEEKLY TOTAL MILES _____   TOTAL MINUTES _____
RESTING HR _____   EXERCISING HR _____   WEIGHT _____

WEEKLY PROGRESS MOOD CHART

Moods: 😊 😊 😐 😕 😟

WEEK:

	Beginning Mood	Ending Mood	Strategy Most Successful	Comments
Day				
1				
2				
3				
4				
5				
6				
7				

DAILY LOG

Monday
date

DAILY TOTAL

Tuesday
date

DAILY TOTAL

Wednesday
date

DAILY TOTAL

Thursday
date

DAILY TOTAL

Friday
date

DAILY TOTAL

Saturday
date

DAILY TOTAL

Sunday
date

DAILY TOTAL

WEEKLY TOTAL MILES _____   TOTAL MINUTES _____
RESTING HR _____   EXERCISING HR _____   WEIGHT _____

WEEKLY PROGRESS MOOD CHART

| Moods: | ☺ ☺ 😐 ☹ 😖 |

WEEK:

	Beginning Mood	Ending Mood	Strategy Most Successful	Comments
Day				
1				
2				
3				
4				
5				
6				
7				

Weekly Mood Chart - From, **IN PURSUIT OF EXCELLENCE**, Courtesy of Tom Orlick. © 1990 by Tom Orlick. by permission of Human Kinetics; Champagne, Illinois. Available in books or call **(800) 747-4457**. $15.95 plus S&H

DAILY LOG

Monday
date

DAILY TOTAL

Tuesday
date

DAILY TOTAL

Wednesday
date

DAILY TOTAL

Thursday
date

DAILY TOTAL

Friday
date

DAILY TOTAL

Saturday
date

DAILY TOTAL

Sunday
date

DAILY TOTAL

WEEKLY TOTAL MILES _____   TOTAL MINUTES _____
RESTING HR _____   EXERCISING HR _____   WEIGHT _____

WEEKLY PROGRESS MOOD CHART

| Moods: | ☺ | ☺ | 😐 | ☹ | 😦 |

WEEK:

	Beginning Mood	Ending Mood	Strategy Most Successful	Comments
Day				
1				
2				
3				
4				
5				
6				
7				

Weekly Mood Chart - From, **IN PURSUIT OF EXCELLENCE**, Courtesy of Tom Orlick. © 1990 by Tom Orlick.
by permission of Human Kinetics; Champagne, Illinois. Available in books or call **(800) 747-4457**. $15.95 plus S&H

DAILY LOG

Monday
date

DAILY TOTAL

Tuesday
date

DAILY TOTAL

Wednesday
date

DAILY TOTAL

Thursday
date

DAILY TOTAL

Friday
date

DAILY TOTAL

Saturday
date

DAILY TOTAL

Sunday
date

DAILY TOTAL

WEEKLY TOTAL MILES _____   TOTAL MINUTES _____
RESTING HR _____   EXERCISING HR _____   WEIGHT _____

WEEKLY PROGRESS MOOD CHART

Moods:	☺ ☺ 😐 ☹ ☹

WEEK:

Day	Beginning Mood	Ending Mood	Strategy Most Successful	Comments
1				
2				
3				
4				
5				
6				
7				

Weekly Mood Chart - From, **IN PURSUIT OF EXCELLENCE**, Courtesy of Tom Orlick. © 1990 by Tom Orlick. by permission of Human Kinetics; Champagne, Illinois. Available in books or call **(800) 747-4457**. $15.95 plus S&H

DAILY LOG

Monday
date

DAILY TOTAL

Tuesday
date

DAILY TOTAL

Wednesday
date

DAILY TOTAL

Thursday
date

DAILY TOTAL

Friday
date

DAILY TOTAL

Saturday
date

DAILY TOTAL

Sunday
date

DAILY TOTAL

WEEKLY TOTAL MILES _____   TOTAL MINUTES _____

RESTING HR _____   EXERCISING HR _____   WEIGHT _____

WEEKLY PROGRESS MOOD CHART

Moods:	☺ ☺ ☺ ☹ ☹

WEEK:

	Beginning Mood	Ending Mood	Strategy Most Successful	Comments
Day				
1				
2				
3				
4				
5				
6				
7				

DAILY LOG

Monday
date

DAILY TOTAL

Tuesday
date

DAILY TOTAL

Wednesday
date

DAILY TOTAL

Thursday
date

DAILY TOTAL

Friday
date

DAILY TOTAL

Saturday
date

DAILY TOTAL

Sunday
date

DAILY TOTAL

WEEKLY TOTAL MILES _____   TOTAL MINUTES _____

RESTING HR _____   EXERCISING HR _____   WEIGHT _____

WEEKLY PROGRESS MOOD CHART

Moods: ☺ ☺ ☺ ☹ ☹

WEEK:

	Beginning Mood	Ending Mood	Strategy Most Successful	Comments
Day				
1				
2				
3				
4				
5				
6				
7				

DAILY LOG

Monday
date

DAILY TOTAL

Tuesday
date

DAILY TOTAL

Wednesday
date

DAILY TOTAL

Thursday
date

DAILY TOTAL

Friday
date

DAILY TOTAL

Saturday
date

DAILY TOTAL

Sunday
date

DAILY TOTAL

WEEKLY TOTAL MILES _____   TOTAL MINUTES _____

RESTING HR _____   EXERCISING HR _____   WEIGHT _____

WEEKLY PROGRESS MOOD CHART

Moods: ☺ ☺ ☺ ☹ ☹

WEEK:

Day	Beginning Mood	Ending Mood	Strategy Most Successful	Comments
1				
2				
3				
4				
5				
6				
7				

DAILY LOG

Monday
date

DAILY TOTAL

Tuesday
date

DAILY TOTAL

Wednesday
date

DAILY TOTAL

Thursday
date

DAILY TOTAL

Friday
date

DAILY TOTAL

Saturday
date

DAILY TOTAL

Sunday
date

DAILY TOTAL

WEEKLY TOTAL MILES _____   TOTAL MINUTES _____
RESTING HR _____   EXERCISING HR _____   WEIGHT _____

WEEKLY PROGRESS MOOD CHART

Moods: ☺   ☺   ☺   ☹   ☹

WEEK:

	Beginning Mood	Ending Mood	Strategy Most Successful	Comments
Day				
1				
2				
3				
4				
5				
6				
7				

Weekly Mood Chart - From, **IN PURSUIT OF EXCELLENCE**, Courtesy of Tom Orlick. © 1990 by Tom Orlick. by permission of Human Kinetics; Champagne, Illinois. Available in books or call **(800) 747-4457.** $15.95 plus S&H

DAILY LOG

Monday
date

DAILY TOTAL

Tuesday
date

DAILY TOTAL

Wednesday
date

DAILY TOTAL

Thursday
date

DAILY TOTAL

Friday
date

DAILY TOTAL

Saturday
date

DAILY TOTAL

Sunday
date

DAILY TOTAL

WEEKLY TOTAL MILES _____   TOTAL MINUTES _____

RESTING HR _____   EXERCISING HR _____   WEIGHT _____

WEEKLY PROGRESS MOOD CHART

Moods: / 😊 😐 😐 😦 😦

WEEK:

Day	Beginning Mood	Ending Mood	Strategy Most Successful	Comments
1				
2				
3				
4				
5				
6				
7				

DAILY LOG

Monday
date

DAILY TOTAL

Tuesday
date

DAILY TOTAL

Wednesday
date

DAILY TOTAL

Thursday
date

DAILY TOTAL

Friday
date

DAILY TOTAL

Saturday
date

DAILY TOTAL

Sunday
date

DAILY TOTAL

WEEKLY TOTAL MILES _____   TOTAL MINUTES _____
         RESTING HR _____   EXERCISING HR _____   WEIGHT _____

WEEKLY PROGRESS MOOD CHART

Moods: ☺ ☺ 😐 ☹ ☹

WEEK:

Day	Beginning Mood	Ending Mood	Strategy Most Successful	Comments
1				
2				
3				
4				
5				
6				
7				

DAILY LOG

Monday
date

DAILY TOTAL

Tuesday
date

DAILY TOTAL

Wednesday
date

DAILY TOTAL

Thursday
date

DAILY TOTAL

Friday
date

DAILY TOTAL

Saturday
date

DAILY TOTAL

Sunday
date

DAILY TOTAL

WEEKLY TOTAL MILES _____   TOTAL MINUTES _____

RESTING HR _____   EXERCISING HR _____   WEIGHT _____

DAILY MOOD CHART

Moods: 😊 🙂 😐 🙁 ☹️

Date: Time Event	Mood Scale	Comments
Start of Practice		
Warm up		
Start		
Mood Change		
End		
Workout		
Start		
Mood Change		
End		
Cool Down		
Start		
Mood Change		
End		
Weight Training		
Start		
Mood Change		
End		
Relaxation/Visual		
Start		
Mood Change		
End		

Date: Time Event	Mood Scale	Comments
Start of Practice		
Warm up		
Start		
Mood Change		
End		
Workout		
Start		
Mood Change		
End		
Cool Down		
Start		
Mood Change		
End		
Weight Training		
Start		
Mood Change		
End		
Relaxation/Visual		
Start		
Mood Change		
End		

DAILY MOOD CHART

Moods:	😊 😐 😑 🙁 ☹️

Date: Time Event	Mood Scale	Comments
Start of Practice		
Warm up		
Start		
Mood Change		
End		
Workout		
Start		
Mood Change		
End		
Cool Down		
Start		
Mood Change		
End		
Weight Training		
Start		
Mood Change		
End		
Relaxation/Visual		
Start		
Mood Change		
End		

Date: Time Event	Mood Scale	Comments
Start of Practice		
Warm up		
Start		
Mood Change		
End		
Workout		
Start		
Mood Change		
End		
Cool Down		
Start		
Mood Change		
End		
Weight Training		
Start		
Mood Change		
End		
Relaxation/Visual		
Start		
Mood Change		
End		

DAILY MOOD CHART

Moods: 😊 😊 😐 🙁 ☹️

Date: Time Event	Mood Scale	Comments
Start of Practice		
Warm up		
Start		
Mood Change		
End		
Workout		
Start		
Mood Change		
End		
Cool Down		
Start		
Mood Change		
End		
Weight Training		
Start		
Mood Change		
End		
Relaxation/Visual		
Start		
Mood Change		
End		

Date: Time Event	Mood Scale	Comments
Start of Practice		
Warm up		
Start		
Mood Change		
End		
Workout		
Start		
Mood Change		
End		
Cool Down		
Start		
Mood Change		
End		
Weight Training		
Start		
Mood Change		
End		
Relaxation/Visual		
Start		
Mood Change		
End		

DAILY MOOD CHART

Moods:	☺ ☺ ☺ ☹ ☹

Date: Time Event	Mood Scale	Comments
Start of Practice		
Warm up		
Start		
Mood Change		
End		
Workout		
Start		
Mood Change		
End		
Cool Down		
Start		
Mood Change		
End		
Weight Training		
Start		
Mood Change		
End		
Relaxation/Visual		
Start		
Mood Change		
End		

Date: Time Event	Mood Scale	Comments
Start of Practice		
Warm up		
Start		
Mood Change		
End		
Workout		
Start		
Mood Change		
End		
Cool Down		
Start		
Mood Change		
End		
Weight Training		
Start		
Mood Change		
End		
Relaxation/Visual		
Start		
Mood Change		
End		

DAILY MOOD CHART

Moods: 😊 😊 😐 🙁 ☹️

Date: Time Event	Mood Scale	Comments
Start of Practice		
Warm up		
Start		
Mood Change		
End		
Workout		
Start		
Mood Change		
End		
Cool Down		
Start		
Mood Change		
End		
Weight Training		
Start		
Mood Change		
End		
Relaxation/Visual		
Start		
Mood Change		
End		

Date: Time Event	Mood Scale	Comments
Start of Practice		
Warm up		
Start		
Mood Change		
End		
Workout		
Start		
Mood Change		
End		
Cool Down		
Start		
Mood Change		
End		
Weight Training		
Start		
Mood Change		
End		
Relaxation/Visual		
Start		
Mood Change		
End		

DAILY MOOD CHART

Moods: 😊 😊 😊 ☹️ ☹️

Date: Time Event	Mood Scale	Comments
Start of Practice		
Warm up		
Start		
Mood Change		
End		
Workout		
Start		
Mood Change		
End		
Cool Down		
Start		
Mood Change		
End		
Weight Training		
Start		
Mood Change		
End		
Relaxation/Visual		
Start		
Mood Change		
End		

Date: Time Event	Mood Scale	Comments
Start of Practice		
Warm up		
Start		
Mood Change		
End		
Workout		
Start		
Mood Change		
End		
Cool Down		
Start		
Mood Change		
End		
Weight Training		
Start		
Mood Change		
End		
Relaxation/Visual		
Start		
Mood Change		
End		

DAILY MOOD CHART

| Moods: | ☺ ☺ ☺ ☹ ☹ |

Date: Time Event	Mood Scale	Comments
Start of Practice		
Warm up		
Start		
Mood Change		
End		
Workout		
Start		
Mood Change		
End		
Cool Down		
Start		
Mood Change		
End		
Weight Training		
Start		
Mood Change		
End		
Relaxation/Visual		
Start		
Mood Change		
End		

Date: Time Event	Mood Scale	Comments
Start of Practice		
Warm up		
Start		
Mood Change		
End		
Workout		
Start		
Mood Change		
End		
Cool Down		
Start		
Mood Change		
End		
Weight Training		
Start		
Mood Change		
End		
Relaxation/Visual		
Start		
Mood Change		
End		

DAILY MOOD CHART

Moods:	😊 😊 😐 🙁 🙁

Date: Time Event	Mood Scale	Comments
Start of Practice		
Warm up		
Start		
Mood Change		
End		
Workout		
Start		
Mood Change		
End		
Cool Down		
Start		
Mood Change		
End		
Weight Training		
Start		
Mood Change		
End		
Relaxation/Visual		
Start		
Mood Change		
End		

Date: Time Event	Mood Scale	Comments
Start of Practice		
Warm up		
Start		
Mood Change		
End		
Workout		
Start		
Mood Change		
End		
Cool Down		
Start		
Mood Change		
End		
Weight Training		
Start		
Mood Change		
End		
Relaxation/Visual		
Start		
Mood Change		
End		

DAILY MOOD CHART

Moods: 😊 😊 😐 🙁 😣

Date: Time Event	Mood Scale	Comments
Start of Practice		
Warm up		
Start		
Mood Change		
End		
Workout		
Start		
Mood Change		
End		
Cool Down		
Start		
Mood Change		
End		
Weight Training		
Start		
Mood Change		
End		
Relaxation/Visual		
Start		
Mood Change		
End		

Date: Time Event	Mood Scale	Comments
Start of Practice		
Warm up		
Start		
Mood Change		
End		
Workout		
Start		
Mood Change		
End		
Cool Down		
Start		
Mood Change		
End		
Weight Training		
Start		
Mood Change		
End		
Relaxation/Visual		
Start		
Mood Change		
End		

DAILY MOOD CHART

Moods: 🙂 🙂 😐 🙁 🙁

Date: Time Event	Mood Scale	Comments
Start of Practice		
Warm up		
Start		
Mood Change		
End		
Workout		
Start		
Mood Change		
End		
Cool Down		
Start		
Mood Change		
End		
Weight Training		
Start		
Mood Change		
End		
Relaxation/Visual		
Start		
Mood Change		
End		

Date: Time Event	Mood Scale	Comments
Start of Practice		
Warm up		
Start		
Mood Change		
End		
Workout		
Start		
Mood Change		
End		
Cool Down		
Start		
Mood Change		
End		
Weight Training		
Start		
Mood Change		
End		
Relaxation/Visual		
Start		
Mood Change		
End		

DAILY MOOD CHART

Moods: ☺ ☺ ☺ ☹ ☹

Date: Time Event	Mood Scale	Comments
Start of Practice		
Warm up		
Start		
Mood Change		
End		
Workout		
Start		
Mood Change		
End		
Cool Down		
Start		
Mood Change		
End		
Weight Training		
Start		
Mood Change		
End		
Relaxation/Visual		
Start		
Mood Change		
End		

Date: Time Event	Mood Scale	Comments
Start of Practice		
Warm up		
Start		
Mood Change		
End		
Workout		
Start		
Mood Change		
End		
Cool Down		
Start		
Mood Change		
End		
Weight Training		
Start		
Mood Change		
End		
Relaxation/Visual		
Start		
Mood Change		
End		

DAILY MOOD CHART

Moods: 😊 😊 😐 🙁 🙁

Date: Time Event	Mood Scale	Comments
Start of Practice		
Warm up		
Start		
Mood Change		
End		
Workout		
Start		
Mood Change		
End		
Cool Down		
Start		
Mood Change		
End		
Weight Training		
Start		
Mood Change		
End		
Relaxation/Visual		
Start		
Mood Change		
End		

Date: Time Event	Mood Scale	Comments
Start of Practice		
Warm up		
Start		
Mood Change		
End		
Workout		
Start		
Mood Change		
End		
Cool Down		
Start		
Mood Change		
End		
Weight Training		
Start		
Mood Change		
End		
Relaxation/Visual		
Start		
Mood Change		
End		

DAILY MOOD CHART

| Moods: | ☺ ☺ ☺ ☹ ☹ |

Date: Time Event	Mood Scale	Comments
Start of Practice		
Warm up		
Start		
Mood Change		
End		
Workout		
Start		
Mood Change		
End		
Cool Down		
Start		
Mood Change		
End		
Weight Training		
Start		
Mood Change		
End		
Relaxation/Visual		
Start		
Mood Change		
End		

Date: Time Event	Mood Scale	Comments
Start of Practice		
Warm up		
Start		
Mood Change		
End		
Workout		
Start		
Mood Change		
End		
Cool Down		
Start		
Mood Change		
End		
Weight Training		
Start		
Mood Change		
End		
Relaxation/Visual		
Start		
Mood Change		
End		

DAILY MOOD CHART

Moods: ☺ ☺ 😐 🙁 ☹

Date: Time Event	Mood Scale	Comments
Start of Practice		
Warm up		
Start		
Mood Change		
End		
Workout		
Start		
Mood Change		
End		
Cool Down		
Start		
Mood Change		
End		
Weight Training		
Start		
Mood Change		
End		
Relaxation/Visual		
Start		
Mood Change		
End		

Date: Time Event	Mood Scale	Comments
Start of Practice		
Warm up		
Start		
Mood Change		
End		
Workout		
Start		
Mood Change		
End		
Cool Down		
Start		
Mood Change		
End		
Weight Training		
Start		
Mood Change		
End		
Relaxation/Visual		
Start		
Mood Change		
End		

DAILY MOOD CHART

Moods: 😊 😊 😐 🙁 ☹️

Date: Time Event	Mood Scale	Comments
Start of Practice		
Warm up		
Start		
Mood Change		
End		
Workout		
Start		
Mood Change		
End		
Cool Down		
Start		
Mood Change		
End		
Weight Training		
Start		
Mood Change		
End		
Relaxation/Visual		
Start		
Mood Change		
End		

Date: Time Event	Mood Scale	Comments
Start of Practice		
Warm up		
Start		
Mood Change		
End		
Workout		
Start		
Mood Change		
End		
Cool Down		
Start		
Mood Change		
End		
Weight Training		
Start		
Mood Change		
End		
Relaxation/Visual		
Start		
Mood Change		
End		

DAILY MOOD CHART

Moods:	😊 😊 😐 🙁 😣

Date: Time Event	Mood Scale	Comments
Start of Practice		
Warm up		
Start		
Mood Change		
End		
Workout		
Start		
Mood Change		
End		
Cool Down		
Start		
Mood Change		
End		
Weight Training		
Start		
Mood Change		
End		
Relaxation/Visual		
Start		
Mood Change		
End		

Date: Time Event	Mood Scale	Comments
Start of Practice		
Warm up		
Start		
Mood Change		
End		
Workout		
Start		
Mood Change		
End		
Cool Down		
Start		
Mood Change		
End		
Weight Training		
Start		
Mood Change		
End		
Relaxation/Visual		
Start		
Mood Change		
End		

DAILY MOOD CHART

Moods: ☺ ☺ 😐 ☹ ☹

Date: Time Event	Mood Scale	Comments
Start of Practice		
Warm up		
Start		
Mood Change		
End		
Workout		
Start		
Mood Change		
End		
Cool Down		
Start		
Mood Change		
End		
Weight Training		
Start		
Mood Change		
End		
Relaxation/Visual		
Start		
Mood Change		
End		

Date: Time Event	Mood Scale	Comments
Start of Practice		
Warm up		
Start		
Mood Change		
End		
Workout		
Start		
Mood Change		
End		
Cool Down		
Start		
Mood Change		
End		
Weight Training		
Start		
Mood Change		
End		
Relaxation/Visual		
Start		
Mood Change		
End		

DAILY MOOD CHART

Moods: 🙂 🙂 😐 🙁 ☹️

Date: Time Event	Mood Scale	Comments
Start of Practice		
Warm up		
Start		
Mood Change		
End		
Workout		
Start		
Mood Change		
End		
Cool Down		
Start		
Mood Change		
End		
Weight Training		
Start		
Mood Change		
End		
Relaxation/Visual		
Start		
Mood Change		
End		

Date: Time Event	Mood Scale	Comments
Start of Practice		
Warm up		
Start		
Mood Change		
End		
Workout		
Start		
Mood Change		
End		
Cool Down		
Start		
Mood Change		
End		
Weight Training		
Start		
Mood Change		
End		
Relaxation/Visual		
Start		
Mood Change		
End		

DAILY MOOD CHART

Moods: 😊 😊 😐 🙁 😣

Date: Time Event	Mood Scale	Comments
Start of Practice		
Warm up		
Start		
Mood Change		
End		
Workout		
Start		
Mood Change		
End		
Cool Down		
Start		
Mood Change		
End		
Weight Training		
Start		
Mood Change		
End		
Relaxation/Visual		
Start		
Mood Change		
End		

Date: Time Event	Mood Scale	Comments
Start of Practice		
Warm up		
Start		
Mood Change		
End		
Workout		
Start		
Mood Change		
End		
Cool Down		
Start		
Mood Change		
End		
Weight Training		
Start		
Mood Change		
End		
Relaxation/Visual		
Start		
Mood Change		
End		

DAILY MOOD CHART

Moods: ☺ ☺ ☺ ☹ ☹

Date: Time Event	Mood Scale	Comments
Start of Practice		
Warm up		
Start		
Mood Change		
End		
Workout		
Start		
Mood Change		
End		
Cool Down		
Start		
Mood Change		
End		
Weight Training		
Start		
Mood Change		
End		
Relaxation/Visual		
Start		
Mood Change		
End		

Date: Time Event	Mood Scale	Comments
Start of Practice		
Warm up		
Start		
Mood Change		
End		
Workout		
Start		
Mood Change		
End		
Cool Down		
Start		
Mood Change		
End		
Weight Training		
Start		
Mood Change		
End		
Relaxation/Visual		
Start		
Mood Change		
End		

DAILY MOOD CHART

Moods:	😊 😊 😐 🙁 🙁

Date: Time Event	Mood Scale	Comments
Start of Practice		
Warm up		
Start		
Mood Change		
End		
Workout		
Start		
Mood Change		
End		
Cool Down		
Start		
Mood Change		
End		
Weight Training		
Start		
Mood Change		
End		
Relaxation/Visual		
Start		
Mood Change		
End		

Date: Time Event	Mood Scale	Comments
Start of Practice		
Warm up		
Start		
Mood Change		
End		
Workout		
Start		
Mood Change		
End		
Cool Down		
Start		
Mood Change		
End		
Weight Training		
Start		
Mood Change		
End		
Relaxation/Visual		
Start		
Mood Change		
End		

DAILY MOOD CHART

Moods:	☺ ☺ 😐 🙁 🙁

Date: Time Event	Mood Scale	Comments
Start of Practice		
Warm up		
Start		
Mood Change		
End		
Workout		
Start		
Mood Change		
End		
Cool Down		
Start		
Mood Change		
End		
Weight Training		
Start		
Mood Change		
End		
Relaxation/Visual		
Start		
Mood Change		
End		

Date: Time Event	Mood Scale	Comments
Start of Practice		
Warm up		
Start		
Mood Change		
End		
Workout		
Start		
Mood Change		
End		
Cool Down		
Start		
Mood Change		
End		
Weight Training		
Start		
Mood Change		
End		
Relaxation/Visual		
Start		
Mood Change		
End		

DAILY MOOD CHART

Moods: 😊 😊 😐 🙁 😟

Date: Time Event	Mood Scale	Comments
Start of Practice		
Warm up		
Start		
Mood Change		
End		
Workout		
Start		
Mood Change		
End		
Cool Down		
Start		
Mood Change		
End		
Weight Training		
Start		
Mood Change		
End		
Relaxation/Visual		
Start		
Mood Change		
End		

Date: Time Event	Mood Scale	Comments
Start of Practice		
Warm up		
Start		
Mood Change		
End		
Workout		
Start		
Mood Change		
End		
Cool Down		
Start		
Mood Change		
End		
Weight Training		
Start		
Mood Change		
End		
Relaxation/Visual		
Start		
Mood Change		
End		

DAILY MOOD CHART

Moods:	😊 😐 😐 🙁 🙁

Date: Time Event	Mood Scale	Comments
Start of Practice		
Warm up		
Start		
Mood Change		
End		
Workout		
Start		
Mood Change		
End		
Cool Down		
Start		
Mood Change		
End		
Weight Training		
Start		
Mood Change		
End		
Relaxation/Visual		
Start		
Mood Change		
End		

Date: Time Event	Mood Scale	Comments
Start of Practice		
Warm up		
Start		
Mood Change		
End		
Workout		
Start		
Mood Change		
End		
Cool Down		
Start		
Mood Change		
End		
Weight Training		
Start		
Mood Change		
End		
Relaxation/Visual		
Start		
Mood Change		
End		

DAILY MOOD CHART

Moods: 😊 😊 😐 🙁 😟

Date: Time Event	Mood Scale	Comments
Start of Practice		
Warm up		
Start		
Mood Change		
End		
Workout		
Start		
Mood Change		
End		
Cool Down		
Start		
Mood Change		
End		
Weight Training		
Start		
Mood Change		
End		
Relaxation/Visual		
Start		
Mood Change		
End		

Date: Time Event	Mood Scale	Comments
Start of Practice		
Warm up		
Start		
Mood Change		
End		
Workout		
Start		
Mood Change		
End		
Cool Down		
Start		
Mood Change		
End		
Weight Training		
Start		
Mood Change		
End		
Relaxation/Visual		
Start		
Mood Change		
End		

DAILY MOOD CHART

| Moods: | ☺ | ☺ | ☺ | ☹ | ☹ |

Date: Time Event	Mood Scale	Comments
Start of Practice		
Warm up		
Start		
Mood Change		
End		
Workout		
Start		
Mood Change		
End		
Cool Down		
Start		
Mood Change		
End		
Weight Training		
Start		
Mood Change		
End		
Relaxation/Visual		
Start		
Mood Change		
End		

Date: Time Event	Mood Scale	Comments
Start of Practice		
Warm up		
Start		
Mood Change		
End		
Workout		
Start		
Mood Change		
End		
Cool Down		
Start		
Mood Change		
End		
Weight Training		
Start		
Mood Change		
End		
Relaxation/Visual		
Start		
Mood Change		
End		

Exerpted from the Big Red Book, courtesy of Track and Field News, Mountainview CA

10,000M EVEN PACE (64–70s Laps)

Laps	64	64.5	65	65.5	66	66.5	67	67.5	68	68.5	69	69.5	70	Distance
2	2:08	2:09	2:10	2:11	2:12	2:13	2:14	2:15	2:16	2:17	2:18	2:19	2:20	800m
3	3:12	3:14	3:15	3:16	3:18	3:20	3:21	3:22	3:24	3:26	3:27	3:28	3:30	1200m
4	4:16	4:18	4:20	4:22	4:24	4:26	4:28	4:30	4:32	4:34	4:36	4:38	4:40	1600m
5	5:20	5:22	5:25	5:28	5:30	5:32	5:35	5:38	5:40	5:42	5:45	5:48	5:50	2000m
6	6:24	6:27	6:30	6:33	6:36	6:39	6:42	6:45	6:48	6:51	6:54	6:57	7:00	2400m
7	7:28	7:32	7:35	7:38	7:42	7:46	7:49	7:52	7:56	7:60	8:03	8:06	8:10	2800m
7.5	8:00	8:04	8:08	8:11	8:15	8:19	8:22	8:26	8:30	8:34	8:38	8:41	8:45	3000m
8	8:32	8:36	8:40	8:44	8:48	8:52	8:56	9:00	9:04	9:08	9:12	9:16	9:20	3200m
9	9:36	9:40	9:45	9:50	9:54	9:58	10:03	10:08	10:12	10:16	10:21	10:26	10:30	3600m
10	10:40	10:45	10:50	10:55	11:00	11:05	11:10	11:15	11:20	11:25	11:30	11:35	11:40	4000m
11	11:44	11:50	11:55	12:00	12:06	12:12	12:17	12:22	12:28	12:34	12:39	12:44	12:50	4400m
12	12:48	12:54	13:00	13:06	13:12	13:18	13:24	13:30	13:36	13:42	13:48	13:54	14:00	4800m
12.5	13:20	13:26	13:32	13:39	13:45	13:51	13:58	14:04	14:10	14:16	14:22	14:29	14:35	5000m
13	13:52	13:58	14:05	14:12	14:18	14:24	14:31	14:38	14:44	14:50	14:57	15:04	15:10	5200m
14	14:56	15:03	15:10	15:17	15:24	15:31	15:38	15:45	15:52	15:59	16:06	16:13	16:20	5600m
15	16:00	16:08	16:15	16:22	16:30	16:38	16:45	16:52	17:00	17:08	17:15	17:22	17:30	6000m
16	17:04	17:12	17:20	17:28	17:36	17:44	17:52	18:00	18:08	18:16	18:24	18:32	18:40	6400m
17	18:08	18:16	18:25	18:34	18:42	18:50	18:59	19:08	19:16	19:24	19:33	19:42	19:50	6800m
18	19:12	19:21	19:30	19:39	19:48	19:57	20:06	20:15	20:24	20:33	20:42	20:51	21:00	7200m
19	20:16	20:26	20:35	20:44	20:54	21:04	21:13	21:22	21:32	21:42	21:51	22:00	22:10	7600m
20	21:20	21:30	21:40	21:50	22:00	22:10	22:20	22:30	22:40	22:50	23:00	23:10	23:20	8000m
21	22:24	22:34	22:45	22:56	23:06	23:16	23:27	23:38	23:48	23:58	24:09	24:20	24:30	8400m
22	23:28	23:39	23:50	24:01	24:12	24:23	24:34	24:45	24:56	25:07	25:18	25:29	25:40	8800m
23	24:32	24:44	24:55	25:06	25:18	25:30	25:41	25:52	26:04	26:16	26:27	26:38	26:50	9200m
24	25:36	25:48	26:00	26:12	26:24	26:36	26:48	27:00	27:12	27:24	27:36	27:48	28:00	9600m
25	26:40	26:52	27:05	27:18	27:30	27:42	27:55	28:08	28:20	28:32	28:45	28:58	29:10	10,000m

(Splits given are relevant to 400m tracks only.)

Fox, Edward., (1994). Track & Field News, The Big Red Book, 116-122.

Exerpted from the Big Red Book, courtesy of <u>Track and Field News</u>, Mountainview CA

10,000M EVEN PACE (70.5–76.5s Laps)

Laps	70.5	71	71.5	72	72.5	73	73.5	74	74.5	75	75.5	76	76.5	Distance
2	2:21	2:22	2:23	2:24	2:25	2:26	2:27	2:28	2:29	2:30	2:31	2:32	2:33	800m
3	3:32	3:33	3:34	3:36	3:38	3:39	3:40	3:42	3:44	3:45	3:46	3:48	3:50	1200m
4	4:42	4:44	4:46	4:48	4:50	4:52	4:54	4:56	4:58	5:00	5:02	5:04	5:06	1600m
5	5:52	5:55	5:58	6:00	6:02	6:05	6:08	6:10	6:12	6:15	6:18	6:20	6:22	2000m
6	7:03	7:06	7:09	7:12	7:15	7:18	7:21	7:24	7:27	7:30	7:33	7:36	7:39	2400m
7	8:14	8:17	8:20	8:24	8:28	8:31	8:34	8:38	8:42	8:45	8:48	8:52	8:56	2800m
7.5	8:49	8:52	8:56	9:00	9:04	9:08	9:11	9:15	9:19	9:22	9:26	9:30	9:34	3000m
8	9:24	9:28	9:32	9:36	9:40	9:44	9:48	9:52	9:56	10:00	10:04	10:08	10:12	3200m
9	10:34	10:39	10:44	10:48	10:52	10:57	11:02	11:06	11:10	11:15	11:20	11:24	11:28	3600m
10	11:45	11:50	11:55	12:00	12:05	12:10	12:15	12:20	12:25	12:30	12:35	12:40	12:45	4000m
11	12:56	13:01	13:06	13:12	13:18	13:23	13:28	13:34	13:40	13:45	13:50	13:56	14:02	4400m
12	14:06	14:12	14:18	14:24	14:30	14:36	14:42	14:48	14:54	15:00	15:06	15:12	15:18	4800m
12.5	14:41	14:48	14:54	15:00	15:06	15:12	15:19	15:25	15:31	15:38	15:44	15:50	15:56	5000m
13	15:16	15:23	15:30	15:36	15:42	15:49	15:56	16:02	16:08	16:15	16:22	16:28	16:34	5200m
14	16:27	16:34	16:41	16:48	16:55	17:02	17:09	17:16	17:23	17:30	17:37	17:44	17:51	5600m
15	17:38	17:45	17:52	18:00	18:08	18:15	18:22	18:30	18:38	18:45	18:52	19:00	19:08	6000m
16	18:48	18:56	19:04	19:12	19:20	19:28	19:36	19:44	19:52	20:00	20:08	20:16	20:24	6400m
17	19:58	20:07	20:16	20:24	20:32	20:41	20:50	20:58	21:06	21:15	21:24	21:32	21:40	6800m
18	21:09	21:18	21:27	21:36	21:45	21:54	22:03	22:12	22:21	22:30	22:39	22:48	22:57	7200m
19	22:20	22:29	22:38	22:48	22:58	23:07	23:16	23:26	23:36	23:45	23:54	24:04	24:14	7600m
20	23:30	23:40	23:50	24:00	24:10	24:20	24:30	24:40	24:50	25:00	25:10	25:20	25:30	8000m
21	24:40	24:51	25:02	25:12	25:22	25:33	25:44	25:54	26:04	26:15	26:26	26:36	26:46	8400m
22	25:51	26:02	26:13	26:24	26:35	26:46	26:57	27:08	27:19	27:30	27:41	27:52	28:03	8800m
23	27:02	27:13	27:24	27:36	27:48	27:59	28:10	28:22	28:34	28:45	28:56	29:08	29:20	9200m
24	28:12	28:24	28:36	28:48	29:00	29:12	29:24	29:36	29:48	30:00	30:12	30:24	30:36	9600m
25	29:22	29:35	29:48	30:00	30:12	30:25	30:38	30:50	31:02	31:15	31:28	31:40	31:52	10,000m

(Splits given are relevant to 400m tracks only.)

Exerpted from the Big Red Book, courtesy of <u>Track and Field News</u>, Mountainview CA

10,000M EVEN PACE (77–83s Laps)

Laps	77	77.5	78	78.5	79	79.5	80	80.5	81	81.5	82	82.5	83	Distance
2	2:34	2:35	2:36	2:37	2:38	2:39	2:40	2:41	2:42	2:43	2:44	2:45	2:46	800m
3	3:51	3:52	3:54	3:56	3:57	3:58	4:00	4:02	4:03	4:04	4:06	4:08	4:09	1200m
4	5:08	5:10	5:12	5:14	5:16	5:18	5:20	5:22	5:24	5:26	5:28	5:30	5:32	1600m
5	6:25	6:28	6:30	6:32	6:35	6:38	6:40	6:42	6:45	6:48	6:50	6:52	6:55	2000m
6	7:42	7:45	7:48	7:51	7:54	7:57	8:00	8:03	8:06	8:09	8:12	8:15	8:18	2400m
7	8:59	9:02	9:06	9:010	9:13	9:16	9:20	9:24	9:27	9:30	9:34	9:38	9:41	2800m
7.5	9:38	9:41	9:45	9:49	9:52	9:56	10:00	10:04	10:08	10:11	10:15	10:19	10:22	3000m
8	10:16	10:20	10:24	10:28	10:32	10:36	10:40	10:44	10:48	10:52	10:56	11:00	11:04	3200m
9	11:33	11:38	11:42	11:46	11:51	11:56	12:00	12:04	12:09	12:14	12:18	12:22	12:27	3600m
10	12:50	12:55	13:00	13:05	13:10	13:15	13:20	13:25	13:30	13:35	13:40	13:45	13:50	4000m
11	14:07	14:12	14:18	14:24	14:29	14:34	14:40	14:46	14:51	14:56	15:02	15:08	15:13	4400m
12	15:24	15:30	15:36	15:42	15:48	15:54	16:00	16:06	16:12	16:18	16:24	16:30	16:36	4800m
12.5	16:02	16:09	16:15	16:21	16:28	16:34	16:40	16:46	16:52	16:59	17:05	17:11	17:18	5000m
13	16:41	16:48	16:54	17:00	17:07	17:14	17:20	17:26	17:33	17:40	17:46	17:52	17:59	5200m
14	17:58	18:05	18:12	18:19	18:26	18:33	18:40	18:47	18:54	19:01	19:08	19:15	19:22	5600m
15	19:15	19:22	19:30	19:38	19:45	19:52	20:00	20:08	20:15	20:22	20:30	20:38	20:45	6000m
16	20:32	20:40	20:48	20:56	21:04	21:12	21:20	21:28	21:36	21:44	21:52	22:00	22:08	6400m
17	21:49	21:58	22:06	22:14	22:23	22:32	22:40	22:48	22:57	23:06	23:14	23:22	23:31	6800m
18	23:06	23:15	23:24	23:33	23:42	23:51	24:00	24:09	24:18	24:27	24:36	24:45	24:54	7200m
19	24:23	24:32	24:42	24:52	25:01	25:10	25:20	25:30	25:39	25:48	25:58	26:08	26:17	7600m
20	25:40	25:50	26:00	26:10	26:20	26:30	26:40	26:50	27:00	27:10	27:20	27:30	27:40	8000m
21	26:57	27:08	27:18	27:28	27:39	27:50	28:00	28:10	28:21	28:32	28:42	28:52	29:03	8400m
22	28:14	28:25	28:36	28:47	28:58	29:09	29:20	29:31	29:42	29:53	30:04	30:15	30:26	8800m
23	29:31	29:42	29:54	30:06	30:17	30:28	30:40	30:52	31:03	31:14	31:26	31:38	31:49	9200m
24	30:48	31:00	31:12	31:24	31:36	31:48	32:00	32:12	32:24	32:36	32:48	33:00	33:12	9600m
25	32:05	32:18	32:30	32:42	32:55	33:08	33:20	33:32	33:45	33:58	34:10	34:22	34:35	10,000m

(Splits given are relevant to 400m tracks only.)

Exerpted from the Big Red Book, courtesy of Track and Field News, Mountainview CA

10,000M EVEN PACE (83.5–89.5s Laps)

Laps	83.5	84	84.5	85	85.5	86	86.5	87	87.5	88	88.5	89	89.5	Distance
2	2:47	2:48	2:49	2:50	2:51	2:52	2:53	2:54	2:55	2:56	2:57	2:58	2:59	800m
3	4:10	4:12	4:14	4:15	4:16	4:18	4:20	4:21	4:22	4:24	4:26	4:27	4:28	1200m
4	5:34	5:36	5:38	5:40	5:42	5:44	5:46	5:48	5:50	5:52	5:54	5:56	5:58	1600m
5	6:58	7:00	7:02	7:05	7:08	7:10	7:12	7:15	7:18	7:20	7:22	7:25	7:28	2000m
6	8:21	8:24	8:27	8:30	8:33	8:36	8:39	8:42	8:45	8:48	8:51	8:54	8:57	2400m
7	9:44	9:48	9:52	9:55	9:58	10:02	10:06	10:09	10:12	10:16	10:20	10:23	10:26	2800m
7.5	10:26	10:30	10:34	10:38	10:41	10:45	10:49	10:52	10:56	11:00	11:04	11:08	11:11	3000m
8	11:08	11:12	11:16	11:20	11:24	11:28	11:32	11:36	11:40	11:44	11:48	11:52	11:56	3200m
9	12:32	12:36	12:40	12:45	12:50	12:54	12:58	13:03	13:08	13:12	13:16	13:21	13:26	3600m
10	13:55	14:00	14:05	14:10	14:15	14:20	14:25	14:30	14:35	14:40	14:45	14:50	14:55	4000m
11	15:18	15:24	15:30	15:35	15:40	15:46	15:52	15:57	16:02	16:08	16:14	16:19	16:24	4400m
12	16:42	16:48	16:54	17:00	17:06	17:12	17:18	17:24	17:30	17:36	17:42	17:48	17:54	4800m
12.5	17:24	17:30	17:36	17:42	17:49	17:55	18:01	18:08	18:14	18:20	18:26	18:32	18:39	5000m
13	18:06	18:12	18:18	18:25	18:32	18:38	18:44	18:51	18:58	19:04	19:10	19:17	19:24	5200m
14	19:29	19:36	19:43	19:50	19:57	20:04	20:11	20:18	20:25	20:32	20:39	20:46	20:53	5600m
15	20:52	21:00	21:08	21:15	21:22	21:30	21:38	21:45	21:52	22:00	22:08	22:15	22:22	6000m
16	22:16	22:24	22:32	22:40	22:48	22:56	23:04	23:12	23:20	23:28	23:36	23:44	23:52	6400m
17	23:40	23:48	23:56	24:05	24:14	24:22	24:30	24:39	24:48	24:56	25:04	25:13	25:22	6800m
18	25:03	25:12	25:21	25:30	25:39	25:48	25:57	26:06	26:15	26:24	26:33	26:42	26:51	7200m
19	26:26	26:36	26:46	26:55	27:04	27:14	27:24	27:33	27:42	27:52	28:02	28:11	28:20	7600m
20	27:50	28:00	28:10	28:20	28:30	28:40	28:50	29:00	29:10	29:20	29:30	29:40	29:50	8000m
21	29:14	29:24	29:34	29:45	29:56	30:06	30:16	30:27	30:38	30:48	30:58	31:09	31:20	8400m
22	30:37	30:48	30:59	31:10	31:21	31:32	31:43	31:54	32:05	32:16	32:27	32:38	32:49	8800m
23	32:00	32:12	32:24	32:35	32:46	32:58	33:010	33:21	33:32	33:44	33:56	34:07	34:18	9200m
24	33:24	33:36	33:48	34:00	34:12	34:24	34:36	34:48	35:00	35:12	35:24	35:36	35:48	9600m
25	34:48	35:00	35:12	35:25	35:38	35:50	36:02	36:15	36:28	36:40	36:52	37:05	37:18	10,000m

(Splits given are relevant to 400m tracks only.)

Exerpted from the Big Red Book, courtesy of <u>Track and Field News</u>, Mountainview CA

3000M/5000M EVEN PACE

Laps	70	69	68	67	66	65	64	63	62	61	60	59	58	Distance
2	2:20	2:18	2:16	2:14	2:12	2:10	2:08	2:06	2:04	2:02	2:00	1:58	1:56	800m
3	3:30	3:27	3:24	3:21	3:18	3:15	3:12	3:09	3:06	3:03	3:00	2:57	2:54	1200m
4	4:40	4:36	4:32	4:28	4:24	4:20	4:16	4:12	4:08	4:04	4:00	3:56	3:52	1600m
5	5:50	5:45	5:40	5:35	5:30	5:25	5:20	5:15	5:10	5:05	5:00	4:55	4:50	2000m
6	7:00	6:54	6:48	6:42	6:36	6:30	6:24	6:18	6:12	6:06	6:00	5:54	5:48	2400m
7	8:10	8:03	7:56	7:49	7:42	7:35	7:28	7:21	7:14	7:07	7:00	6:53	6:46	2800m
7.5	8:45	8:38	8:30	8:22	8:15	8:08	8:00	7:52	7:45	7:38	7:30	7:22	7:15	3000m
8	9:20	9:12	9:04	8:56	8:48	8:40	8:32	8:24	8:16	8:08	8:00	7:52	7:44	3200m
9	10:30	10:21	10:12	10:03	9:54	9:45	9:36	9:27	9:18	9:09	9:00	8:51	8:42	3600m
10	11:40	11:30	11:20	11:10	11:00	10:50	10:40	10:30	10:20	10:10	10:00	9:50	9:40	4000m
11	12:50	12:39	12:28	12:17	12:06	11:55	11:44	11:33	11:22	11:11	11:00	10:49	10:38	4400m
12	14:00	13:48	13:36	13:24	13:12	13:00	12:48	12:36	12:24	12:12	12:00	11:48	11:36	4800m
12.5	14:35	14:22	14:10	13:58	13:45	13:32	13:20	13:08	12:55	12:42	12:30	12:18	12:05	5000m

(See 10,000m chart for paces slower than 83 seconds per lap)

Laps	83	82	81	80	79	78	77	76	75	74	73	72	71	Distance
2	2:46	2:44	2:42	2:40	2:38	2:36	2:34	2:32	2:30	2:28	2:26	2:24	2:22	800m
3	4:09	4:06	4:03	4:00	3:57	3:54	3:51	3:48	3:45	3:42	3:39	3:36	3:33	1200m
4	5:32	5:28	5:24	5:20	5:16	5:12	5:08	5:04	5:00	4:56	4:52	4:48	4:44	1600m
5	6:55	6:50	6:45	6:40	6:35	6:30	6:25	6:20	6:15	6:10	6:05	6:00	5:55	2000m
6	8:18	8:12	8:06	8:00	7:54	7:48	7:42	7:36	7:30	7:24	7:18	7:12	7:06	2400m
7	9:41	9:34	9:27	9:20	9:13	9:06	8:59	8:52	8:45	8:38	8:31	8:24	8:17	2800m
7.5	10:22	10:15	10:08	10:00	9:52	9:45	9:38	9:30	9:22	9:15	9:08	9:00	8:52	3000m
8	11:04	10:56	10:48	10:40	10:32	10:24	10:16	10:08	10:00	9:52	9:44	9:36	9:28	3200m
9	12:27	12:18	12:09	12:00	11:51	11:42	11:33	11:24	11:15	11:06	10:57	10:48	10:39	3600m
10	13:50	13:40	13:30	13:20	13:10	13:00	12:50	12:40	12:30	12:20	12:10	12:00	11:50	4000m
11	15:13	15:02	14:51	14:40	14:29	14:18	14:07	13:56	13:45	13:34	13:23	13:12	13:01	4400m
12	16:36	16:24	16:12	16:00	15:48	15:36	15:24	15:12	15:00	14:48	14:36	14:24	14:12	4800m
12.5	17:18	17:05	16:52	16:40	16:28	16:15	16:02	15:50	15:38	15:25	15:12	15:00	14:48	5000m

(Splits given are relevant to 400m tracks only.)

Exerpted from the Big Red Book, courtesty of <u>Track and Field News</u>, Mountainview CA

PER-MILE MARATHON PACE

1M	5M	10M	1/2 Mar.	15M	20M	25M	Marathon
4:45	23:45	47:30	1:02:16	1:11:15	1:35:00	1:58:45	2:04:32
4:50	24:10	48:20	1:03:22	1:12:30	1:36:40	2:00:50	2:06:44
4:55	24:35	49:10	1:04:27	1:13:45	1:38:20	2:02:55	2:08:55
5:00	25:00	50:00	1:05:33	1:15:00	1:40:00	2:05:00	2:11:06
5:05	25:25	50:50	1:06:38	1:16:15	1:41:40	2:07:05	2:13:17
5:10	25:50	51:40	1:07:44	1:17:30	1:43:20	2:09:10	2:15:28
5:15	26:15	52:30	1:08:49	1:18:45	1:45:00	2:11:15	2:17:39
5:20	26:40	53:20	1:09:55	1:20:00	1:46:40	2:13:20	2:19:50
5:25	27:05	54:10	1:11:01	1:21:15	1:48:20	2:15:25	2:22:01
5:30	27:30	55:00	1:12:06	1:22:30	1:50:00	2:17:30	2:24:12
5:35	27:55	55:50	1:13:12	1:23:45	1:51:40	2:19:35	2:26:23
5:40	28:20	56:40	1:14:17	1:25:00	1:53:20	2:21:40	2:28:34
5:45	28:45	57:30	1:15:23	1:26:15	1:55:00	2:23:45	2:30:46
5:50	29:10	58:20	1:16:28	1:27:30	1:56:40	2:25:50	2:32:57
5:55	29:35	59:10	1:17:34	1:28:45	1:58:20	2:27:55	2:35:08
6:00	30:00	1:00:00	1:18:39	1:30:00	2:00:00	2:30:00	2:37:19
6:10	30:50	1:01:40	1:20:51	1:32:30	2:03:20	2:34:10	2:41:41
6:15	31:15	1:02:30	1:21:56	1:33:45	2:05:00	2:36:15	2:43:52
6:20	31:40	1:03:20	1:23:02	1:35:00	2:06:40	2:38:20	2:46:03
6:25	32:05	1:04:10	1:24:07	1:36:15	2:08:20	2:40:25	2:48:14
6:30	32:30	1:05:00	1:25:13	1:37:30	2:10:00	2:42:30	2:50:25
6:35	32:55	1:05:50	1:26:18	1:38:45	2:11:40	2:44:35	2:52:37
6:40	33:20	1:06:40	1:27:24	1:40:00	2:13:20	2:46:40	2:54:48
6:45	33:45	1:07:30	1:28:29	1:41:15	2:15:00	2:48:45	2:56:59
6:50	34:10	1:08:20	1:29:35	1:42:30	2:16:40	2:50:50	2:59:10
6:55	34:35	1:09:10	1:30:40	1:43:45	2:18:20	2:52:55	3:01:21
7:00	35:00	1:10:00	1:31:46	1:45:00	2:20:00	2:55:00	3:03:32
7:05	35:25	1:10:50	1:32:52	1:46:15	2:21:40	2:57:05	3:05:43
7:10	35:50	1:11:40	1:33:57	1:47:30	2:23:20	2:59:10	3:07:54
7:15	36:15	1:12:30	1:35:03	1:48:45	2:25:00	3:01:15	3:10:05
7:20	36:40	1:13:20	1:36:08	1:50:00	2:26:40	3:03:20	3:12:1
7:25	37:05	1:14:10	1:37:14	1:51:15	2:28:20	3:05:25	3:14:27
7:30	37:30	1:15:00	1:38:19	1:52:30	2:30:00	3:07:30	3:16:39
7:35	37:55	1:15:50	1:39:25	1:53:45	2:31:40	3:09:35	3:18:50
7:40	38:20	1:16:40	1:40:30	1:55:00	2:33:20	3:11:40	3:21:01
7:45	38:45	1:17:30	1:41:36	1:56:15	2:35:00	3:13:45	3:23:12
7:50	39:10	1:18:20	1:42:41	1:57:30	2:36:40	3:15:50	3:25:23
7:55	39:35	1:19:10	1:43:47	1:58:45	2:38:20	3:17:55	3:27:34
8:00	40:00	1:20:00	1:44:53	2:00:00	2:40:00	3:20:00	3:29:45
8:05	40:25	1:20:50	1:45:58	2:01:15	2:41:40	3:22:05	3:31:56
8:10	40:50	1:21:40	1:47:04	2:02:30	2:43:20	3:24:10	3:34:07
8:15	41:15	1:22:30	1:48:9	2:03:45	2:45:00	3:26:15	3:36:18
8:20	41:40	1:23:20	1:49:15	2:05:00	2:46:40	3:28:20	3:38:30
8:25	42:05	1:24:10	1:50:20	2:06:15	2:48:20	3:30:25	3:40:41
8:30	42:30	1:25:00	1:51:26	2:07:30	2:50:00	3:32:30	3:42:52

Exerpted from the Big Red Book, courtesty of <u>Track and Field News</u>, Mountainview CA

PER-KILOMETER MARATHON PACE

1km	1M	5km	10km	15km	20km	1/2 Mar.	25km	30km	35km	40km	Marathon
2:55	4:42	14:35	29:10	43:45	58:20	1:01:32	1:12:55	1:27:30	1:42:05	1:56:40	2:03:04
3:00	4:50	15:00	30:00	45:00	1:00:00	1:03:18	1:15:00	1:30:00	1:45:00	2:00:00	2:06:35
3:05	4:58	15:25	30:50	46:15	1:01:40	1:05:03	1:17:05	1:32:30	1:47:55	2:03:20	2:10:06
3:10	5:06	15:50	31:40	47:30	1:03:20	1:06:49	1:19:10	1:35:00	1:50:50	2:06:40	2:13:37
3:15	5:14	16:15	32:30	48:45	1:05:00	1:08:34	1:21:15	1:37:30	1:53:45	2:10:00	2:17:08
3:20	5:22	16:40	33:20	50:00	1:06:40	1:10:19	1:23:20	1:40:00	1:56:40	2:13:20	2:20:39
3:25	5:30	17:05	34:10	51:15	1:08:20	1:12:05	1:25:25	1:42:30	1:59:35	2:16:40	2:24:10
3:30	5:38	17:30	35:00	52:30	1:10:00	1:13:50	1:27:30	1:45:00	2:02:30	2:20:00	2:27:41
3:35	5:46	17:55	35:50	53:45	1:11:40	1:15:36	1:29:35	1:47:30	2:05:25	2:23:20	2:31:12
3:40	5:54	18:20	36:40	55:00	1:13:20	1:17:21	1:31:40	1:50:00	2:08:20	2:26:40	2:34:43
3:45	6:02	18:45	37:30	56:15	1:15:00	1:19:07	1:33:45	1:52:30	2:11:15	2:30:00	2:38:14
3:50	6:10	19:10	38:20	57:30	1:16:40	1:20:52	1:35:50	1:55:00	2:14:10	2:33:20	2:41:45
3:55	6:18	19:35	39:10	58:45	1:18:20	1:22:38	1:37:55	1:57:30	2:17:05	2:36:40	2:45:16
4:00	6:26	20:00	40:00	1:00:00	1:20:00	1:24:23	1:40:00	2:00:00	2:20:00	2:40:00	2:48:47
4:05	6:34	20:25	40:50	1:01:15	1:21:40	1:26:09	1:42:05	2:02:30	2:22:55	2:43:20	2:52:18
4:10	6:42	20:50	41:40	1:02:30	1:23:20	1:27:54	1:44:10	2:05:00	2:25:50	2:46:40	2:55:49
4:15	6:50	21:15	42:30	1:03:45	1:25:00	1:29:40	1:46:15	2:07:30	2:28:45	2:50:00	2:59:20
4:20	6:58	21:40	43:20	1:05:00	1:26:40	1:31:25	1:48:20	2:10:00	2:31:40	2:53:20	3:02:51
4:25	7:06	22:05	44:10	1:06:15	1:28:20	1:33:11	1:50:25	2:12:30	2:34:35	2:56:40	3:06:22
4:30	7:15	22:30	45:00	1:07:30	1:30:00	1:34:56	1:52:30	2:15:00	2:37:30	3:00:00	3:09:53
4:35	7:23	22:55	45:50	1:08:45	1:31:40	1:36:42	1:54:35	2:17:30	2:40:25	3:03:20	3:13:24
4:40	7:31	23:20	46:40	1:10:00	1:33:20	1:38:27	1:56:40	2:20:00	2:43:20	3:06:40	3:16:55
4:45	7:39	23:45	47:30	1:11:15	1:35:00	1:40:13	1:58:45	2:22:30	2:46:15	3:10:00	3:20:26
4:50	7:47	24:10	48:20	1:12:30	1:36:40	1:41:58	2:00:50	2:25:00	2:49:10	3:13:20	3:23:57
4:55	7:55	24:35	49:10	1:13:45	1:38:20	1:43:44	2:02:55	2:27:30	2:52:05	3:16:40	3:27:28
5:00	8:03	25:00	50:00	1:15:00	1:40:00	1:45:29	2:05:00	2:30:00	2:55:00	3:20:00	3:30:59
5:05	8:11	25:25	50:50	1:16:15	1:41:40	1:47:15	2:07:05	2:32:30	2:57:55	3:23:20	3:34:29

References

Benson, H. (1975). The Relaxation Response, 23.

Chase, M.A., Lirgg, C.D., & Feltz, D., L. (1997). Do Coaches' Efficacy Expectations for Their Teams Predict Team Performance. The Sport Psychologist, 11, 8-23.

Fox, Edward, (1995). The Big Red Book. Track and Field News, 116-120.

Garfield, C.A., (1984). Mental Training Techniques of the World's Greatest Athletes. Peak Performance, 108-113.

Gordon, S. (1990). A Mental Skills Training Program for the Western Australian State Cricket Team. The Sport Psychologist, 4, 386-399.

Hardy, C.J., Chase, K. (1990). Relaxation Training, Sport Psychology Training Bulletin, 2-1, 1-7.

Jackson, S., A. (1996). Toward a conceptual understanding of the flow experience in elite athletes. Research Quarterly for Exercise and Sport 67-1, 76-90.

Mallet, C.J., Hanrahan, S.J. (1997). Race Modeling: An Effective Cognitive Strategy for the 100m Sprinter. The Sport Psychologist, 11, 72-85.

Murphy, S. M. (1994). Imagery Intervention in Sport. Medicine and Science in Sport and Exercise, 26-4, 486-494.

Orlick, T. (1980). How to win in sport and life through mental training. In Pursuit of Excellence, 2, 56-60.

Reardon, J. (1992). Learning How to "Go With the Flow" Sport Psychologist, Spring, 54-55.

Reardon, J. (1992) The Three C's of Success, Concentration, Composure, Confidence are Key. Sport Psychologist, Summer, 48-50.

Reardon, J. (1995). Dealing with Stress, Relaxation: A Necessary Skill for Competition. Sport Psychologist, Summer, 48-50.

Surgent, F. (1992). See it, Then Do It, Designing a Mental Imagery Program. Running FitNews, 11-2, 4-5.

Vealey, R.S. (1990). Inner Coaching through Mental Imagery. Sport Psychology Training Bulletin, 2-2, 1-5.

Waller, S. (1995). Sport Peak Performance. Oregon Outdoors Magazine, August/ September, 57-58.

GRID CONCENTRATION EXERCISE

Directions:
Beginning with 00, put a slash through each number in the proper sequence

84	27	51	78	59	52	13	85	61	55
28	60	92	04	97	90	31	57	29	33
32	96	65	39	80	77	49	86	18	70
76	87	71	95	98	81	01	46	88	00
48	82	89	47	35	17	10	42	62	34
44	67	93	11	07	43	72	94	69	56
53	79	05	22	54	74	58	14	91	02
06	68	99	75	26	15	41	66	20	40
50	09	64	08	38	30	36	45	83	24
03	73	21	23	16	37	25	19	12	63

Notes

Notes